HERE I AM.
SEND ME!

Isaiah

N E L S O N
I M P A C T™
Bible Study Series

HERE I AM.
SEND ME!

Isaiah

THOMAS NELSON
Since 1798

NASHVILLE DALLAS MEXICO CITY RIO DE JANEIRO

Published in Nashville, Tennessee, by Thomas Nelson®. Thomas Nelson is a registered trademark of Thomas Nelson, Inc.

Thomas Nelson, Inc., titles may be purchased in bulk for educational, business, fund-raising, or sales promotional use. For information, please e-mail SpecialMarkets@ThomasNelson.com.

Scripture quotations marked THE NEW KING JAMES VERSION. © 1982 by Thomas Nelson, Inc. Used by permission. All rights reserved.

Scripture quotations marked KJV are taken from *The Holy Bible,* The King James Version of the Bible.

Scripture quotations marked NASB are taken from *The Holy Bible,* New American Standard Bible, © 1960, 1977 by the Lockman Foundation.

ISBN 978-1-4185-0609-4

Printed in the United States of America.

A Word from the Publisher...

Be diligent to present yourself approved to God, a worker who does not need to be ashamed, rightly dividing the word of truth.

2 Timothy 2:15 NKJV

We are so glad that you have chosen this study guide to enrich your biblical knowledge and strengthen your walk with God. Inside you will find great information that will deepen your understanding and knowledge of this book of the Bible.

Many tools are included to aid you in your study, including ancient and present-day maps of the Middle East, as well as timelines and charts to help you understand when the book was written and why. You will also benefit from sidebars placed strategically throughout this study guide, designed to give you expanded knowledge of language, theology, culture, and other details regarding the Scripture being studied.

We consider it a joy and a ministry to serve you and teach you through these study guides. May your heart be blessed, your mind expanded, and your spirit lifted as you walk through God's Word.

Blessings,

Edward (Les) Middleton, M.Div.
Editor-in-Chief, Nelson Impact

TIMELINE OF OLD

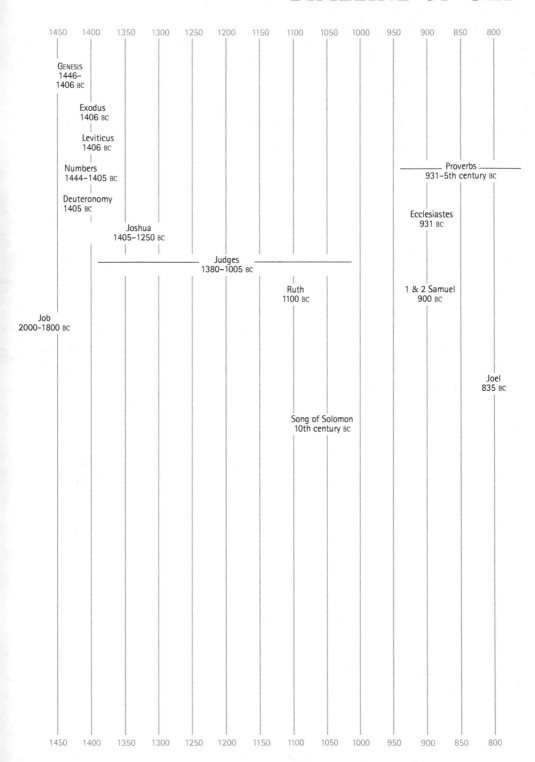

1450 1400 1350 1300 1250 1200 1150 1100 1050 1000 950 900 850 800

GENESIS
1446–
1406 BC

Exodus
1406 BC

Leviticus
1406 BC

Numbers
1444–1405 BC

Deuteronomy
1405 BC

Joshua
1405–1250 BC

Judges
1380–1005 BC

Ruth
1100 BC

Job
2000–1800 BC

Proverbs
931–5th century BC

Ecclesiastes
931 BC

1 & 2 Samuel
900 BC

Joel
835 BC

Song of Solomon
10th century BC

1450 1400 1350 1300 1250 1200 1150 1100 1050 1000 950 900 850 800

TESTAMENT WRITINGS

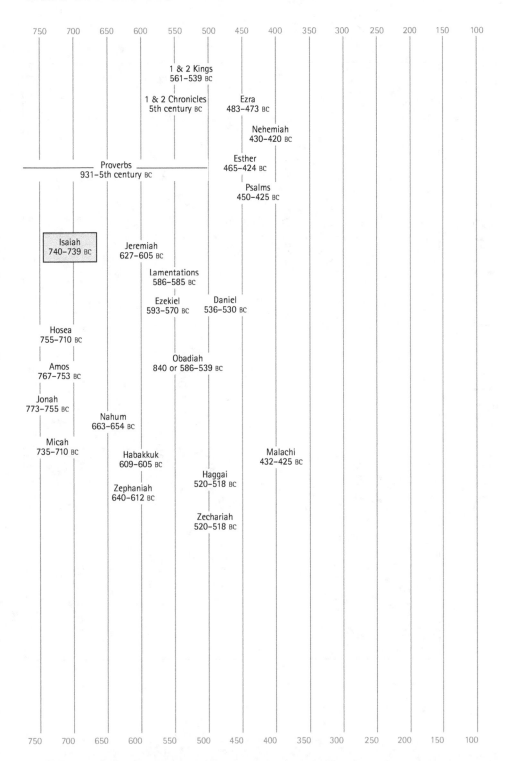

750 700 650 600 550 500 450 400 350 300 250 200 150 100

1 & 2 Kings
561–539 BC

1 & 2 Chronicles   Ezra
5th century BC   483–473 BC

Nehemiah
430–420 BC

Proverbs   Esther
931–5th century BC   465–424 BC

Psalms
450–425 BC

Isaiah   Jeremiah
740–739 BC   627–605 BC

Lamentations
586–585 BC

Ezekiel   Daniel
593–570 BC   536–530 BC

Hosea
755–710 BC

Obadiah
Amos   840 or 586–539 BC
767–753 BC

Jonah
773–755 BC

Nahum
663–654 BC

Micah
735–710 BC   Malachi
Habakkuk   432–425 BC
609–605 BC

Haggai
520–518 BC
Zephaniah
640–612 BC

Zechariah
520–518 BC

750 700 650 600 550 500 450 400 350 300 250 200 150 100

OLD MIDDLE EAST

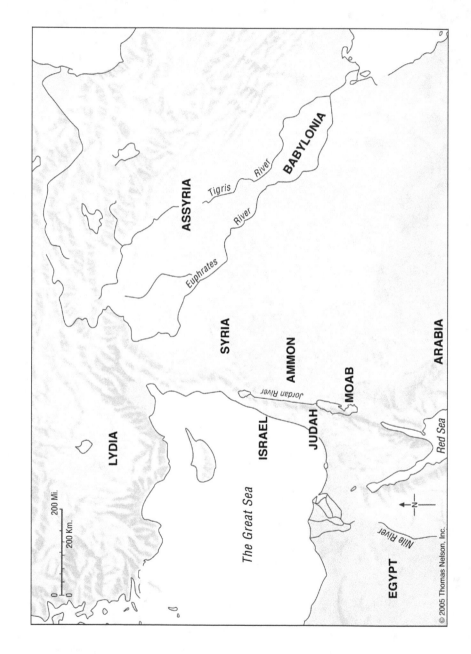

Middle East of Today

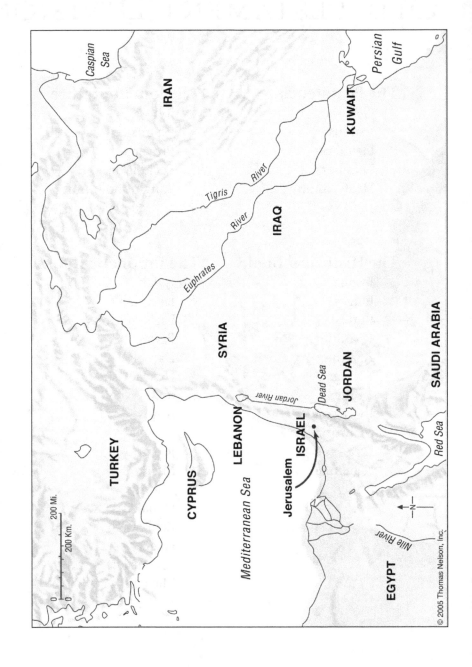

Old Testament Divisions

The Pentateuch
Genesis
Exodus
Leviticus
Numbers
Deuteronomy

Wisdom Literature
Job
Psalms
Proverbs
Ecclesiastes
Song of Solomon

The Historical Books
Joshua
Judges
Ruth
1 Samuel
2 Samuel
1 Kings
2 Kings
1 Chronicles
2 Chronicles
Ezra
Nehemiah
Esther

The Prophetic Books
Isaiah
Jeremiah
Lamentations
Ezekiel
Daniel
Hosea
Joel
Amos
Obadiah
Jonah
Micah
Nahum
Habakkuk
Zephaniah
Haggai
Zechariah
Malachi

New Testament Divisions

The Four Gospels
Matthew
Mark
Luke
John

History
Acts

The Epistles of Paul
Romans
1 Corinthians
2 Corinthians
Galatians
Ephesians
Philippians
Colossians
1 Thessalonians
2 Thessalonians
1 Timothy
2 Timothy
Titus
Philemon

The General Epistles
Hebrews
James
1 Peter
2 Peter
1 John
2 John
3 John
Jude

Apocalyptic Literature
Revelation

ICON KEY

Throughout this study guide, you will find many icon sidebars that will aid and enrich your study of this book of the Bible. To help you identify what these icons represent, please refer to the key below.

BIBLICAL GRAB BAG

A biblical grab bag full of interesting facts and tidbits.

BIBLE

Further exploration of biblical principles and interpretations, along with a little food for thought.

LANGUAGE

Word usages, definitions, interpretations, and information on the Greek and Hebrew languages.

CULTURE

Customs, traditions, and lifestyle practices in biblical times.

ARCHAEOLOGICAL

Archaeological discoveries and artifacts that relate to biblical life, as well as modern-day discoveries.

CONTENTS

INTRODUCTION

O f all the prophetic books in the Bible, none is more beloved and better-known than the book of Isaiah. Consider just a few of its more familiar passages, taken from the King James Version:

Come now, and let us reason together . . . though your sins be as scarlet, they shall be as white as snow . . . (Isa. 1:18).

They shall beat their swords into plowshares, and their spears into pruning-hooks (Isa. 2:4).

Woe unto them that call evil good, and good evil (Isa. 5:20).

The wolf also shall dwell with the lamb, and the leopard shall lie down with the kid; and the calf and the young lion and the fatling together; and a little child shall lead them (Isa. 11:6).

Let us eat and drink; for to morrow we shall die (Isa. 22:13).

But they that wait upon the LORD shall renew their strength; they shall mount up with wings as eagles; they shall run, and not be weary; and they shall walk, and not faint (Isa. 40:31).

Seek ye the LORD while he may be found, call ye upon him while he is near (Isa. 55:6).

For my thoughts are not your thoughts, neither are your ways my ways, saith the LORD (Isa. 55:8).

They make haste to shed innocent blood (Isa. 59:7).

*All our righteousnesses are as filthy rags; and we all do
fade as a leaf (Isa. 64:6).*

WHERE DID HANDEL GET HIS WORDS?

If you have ever participated in—or listened to—a performance
of Handel's *Messiah,* you know the majesty of both the music and the words.
Handel and his librettist, Charles Jennens, used fifty-nine quotations from the
Bible to tell the story. Of these fifty-nine, seventeen came from the book of
Isaiah—almost 30 percent of the total. These include such familiar recitatives and
arias as "Comfort ye," "Every valley shall be exalted," "And the glory of the Lord,"
and "All we like sheep have gone astray." (See also "A True Treasure Trove" on page
80 of this study guide.)

It would be a simple matter to find another twenty or thirty
passages from Isaiah that are just as familiar as the above.
Undoubtedly we shall do so in the pages ahead. But first, a few
words of introduction . . .

THE AUTHOR AND HIS TIME

The author of the book of Isaiah is a man whose Hebrew
name would be transliterated as *Yesha'Yahu,* meaning
"Yahweh is salvation." We know him, of course, as Isaiah, who
makes it plain in the very first verse that his book is

*the vision of Isaiah the son of Amoz, which he saw
concerning Judah and Jerusalem in the days of Uzziah,
Jotham, Ahaz, and Hezekiah, kings of Judah (Isa. 1:1
NKJV).*

Isaiah is generally considered the one and only author of his
own book, although some scholars have suggested that as

many as two other writers might have been involved. However, both outside evidence and the linguistic and stylistic evidence within the book itself strongly imply that Isaiah had but one source. For example, in terms of external evidence, the Dead Sea Scrolls (dating to the second century BC) include a complete copy of Isaiah as one book. Also, Isaiah is referenced by name twenty-one separate times in the New Testament, and quotations credited to him come from both the early chapters (1–39) and the later ones (40–66).

In terms of internal evidence, the expression "the Holy One of Israel" occurs twenty-six times throughout the book of Isaiah, but only six additional times in the entire Old Testament. Likewise, the theological unity is consistent throughout the book, again suggesting just one author.

WHAT IS A PROPHET?

Many people believe that a prophet is one who tells the future. While this is sometimes true, the original Hebrew word for "prophet," *Navi,* meant "to bubble forth as from a fountain," or "to utter." According to ancient Hebrew understanding, a prophet was thus an intermediary between God and His people—one who "bubbled forth" the words of God, whether they involved the future or the present. Indeed, although Isaiah certainly did speak of the distant future, he also spent a great deal of time dealing with the current realities of his day, repeatedly warning the people of Judah (including four different kings) of the immediate consequences of their actions.

The very first verse, quoted above, also places Isaiah's work in a clear historical context. The four kings he named, starting with Uzziah and ending with Hezekiah, reigned from 790 to 686 BC, during a time when the nation of Israel was clearly sliding downhill, especially in spiritual terms. However, Isaiah also wrote about the death of Sennacherib (Isa. 37:38), one of the best-known kings of the Assyrian empire, which occurred in 681 BC. On the other hand, Uzziah died in 739 BC. These two dates, taken together, tell us that Isaiah occupied his office

What Was the "Southern" vs. the "Northern" Kingdom?

When God established the nation of Israel, He did not intend for it ever to be divided. In fact, He really didn't intend for it to have earthly kings—the system of judges that persisted for several years after Moses died, with God Himself as the true King of Israel and a series of judges to execute His commands, was undoubtedly God's original plan. But eventually, when Samuel grew old and his sons were about to become judges, the people clamored for a king instead, as shown in 1 Samuel 8:7–9 (NKJV):

> And the LORD said to Samuel, "Heed the voice of the people in all that they say to you; for they have not rejected you, but they have rejected Me, that I should not reign over them. According to all the works which they have done since the day that I brought them up out of Egypt, even to this day—with which they have forsaken Me and served other gods—so they are doing to you also. Now therefore, heed their voice. However, you shall solemnly forewarn them, and show them the behavior of the king who will reign over them."

Saul then became Israel's first king, followed by David, then by Solomon. Unfortunately, when Solomon died and his son Rehoboam came into power, he so angered the people (by his harsh treatment, inspired by young, inexperienced advisors) that the northern portion of the kingdom rebelled, broke off, and crowned Jeroboam, Solomon's servant, as their king instead. From that point on the Northern Kingdom was known as Israel, and the Southern Kingdom, which retained the capital city of Jerusalem, was known as Judah.

What's most important to remember from all this, however, is that Israel was (1) the name given by God to Jacob; then (2) the name given to the nation founded by the twelve sons of Jacob/Israel; then (3) the name given to the Northern Kingdom when Israel split into two pieces; and then (4) the name essentially restored to the remnant of survivors who returned to Jerusalem after the Babylonian captivity and basically reestablished the independent nation of Israel (which we sometimes call the children of Israel).

However, when Isaiah was writing to the people of the Southern Kingdom, which still existed as a separate entity in his time, he addressed them collectively (and correctly, for that era) as Judah. Even so, via the process detailed above, the word *Israel* eventually came back into general usage to mean the collective body of legitimate descendants from any of the original twelve tribes of Israel, plus any "aliens" who were "grafted in" to the nation of Israel in the manner prescribed by God Himself when He brought Israel out of Egypt (see the book of Exodus).

Given all that, in this study guide we may sometimes use Israel, or Judah (or sometimes Judah/Israel when referencing Isaiah's own words) to refer to the nation of Israel as described above.

as prophet for at least fifty-eight years, and probably some-what longer, depending on when (during Uzziah's reign) he began his ministry.

Isaiah prophesied during a time of great trouble for the nation of Israel. The Northern Kingdom (called "Israel") was con-quered by Assyria in 722 BC. This left the Southern Kingdom (called "Judah") to stand on its own for another 136 years, until it finally fell to the Babylonians in 586 BC, thus begin-ning seventy years in captivity. Isaiah knew what was coming, and even though he did not live to see Judah's final days, he felt plenty of sorrow over what lay ahead.

Isaiah was married and had two sons, both of whom he men-tions by name—Shear-Jashub in 7:3 and Maher-Shalal-Hash-Baz in 8:3. Hebrew tradition also suggests that Isaiah himself was a cousin of King Uzziah, but this has never been proven.

WHY DID THE BABYLONIANS WIN?

The Babylonian captivity, about which Isaiah had so much to say, lasted exactly seventy years. During this time, the land of Israel was abandoned to lie fallow. However, those seventy years were not the least bit arbitrary. In Leviticus 25:1–5, God instructed Moses to institute a sabbath for the land, meaning that during every seventh year His people were to grow no crops at all, but to let the land rest and restore itself. Unfortunately, during the 800 years they were in the land of Canaan, for a cumulative period of time equal to 490 years, the children of Israel failed to observe God's sabbath for the land. Thus the number 70, derived by dividing 490 by 7.

These seventy years were also referred to by the prophet Jeremiah and referenced in the book of 2 Chronicles:

And those who escaped from the sword he [the king of the Chaldeans] car-ried away to Babylon, where they became servants to him and his sons until the rule of the kingdom of Persia, to fulfill the word of the LORD by the mouth of Jeremiah, until the land had enjoyed her Sabbaths. As long as she lay des-olate she kept Sabbath, to fulfill seventy years. (2 Chr. 36:20–21 NKJV)

JUDGMENT AND REDEMPTION

It is not an easy matter to extract a single, all-encompassing theme from the entire message of Isaiah. Instead, most scholars break the book down into two major sections with corresponding themes, one leading directly into the other.

Section one, which includes chapters 1–39, is largely about judgment. This lines up very clearly with what Moses wrote in Deuteronomy—that God would first execute judgment upon Israel for her sin. Section two, which includes chapters 40–66, is largely about redemption, which also lines up with Deuteronomy. First God judges; then He redeems.

On the other hand, much of what Isaiah wrote about the redemptive process did not concern itself with the near future. He had little to say, for example, about the Israelites' return to Jerusalem when the Babylonian captivity ended. Isaiah was much more concerned with real change on a much larger scale—the kind of change that could come about only through the advent of the ultimate Savior of all humankind, Jesus Christ Himself. Thus Isaiah's writings are among the most hope-filled, poetic, and just plain uplifting words in the entire Bible.

Overall, the two thematic sections of Isaiah are organized as follows:

PART 1—THE JUDGMENT OF GOD (CHAPTERS 1–39)

In these thirty-nine chapters, even as Isaiah spoke of punishment from God for the sin of His people, he wrote about blessings as well. Thus it will become clear, as we deal with the chapters of each section in more detail later in this study guide, that the blessings God promised the Israelites via the covenant He put in place through Abraham, Isaac, and Jacob would still be theirs. In other words, even as Isaiah showed how sin must be rooted out and exposed, he also emphasized God's plans to restore Israel and make her a righteous nation once again. His words thus convey both warnings and promises—the first to be heeded, the second to be enjoyed as an assured result, even if not immediate.

Part 2—The Redemption of God (Chapters 40–66)

These twenty-seven chapters focus on three events, all of which were still in the future when Isaiah wrote about them.

First, after her time of suffering was complete, Israel would be redeemed from Babylonia and restored to the land of Israel, via the rebuilding of Jerusalem.

Second, the Suffering Servant (Christ) would be rejected by Israel. But by His sacrificial death, He would still make provision for the redemption of those who believe in Him and do as God's Word makes clear.

Third, the Lord would someday accomplish a far greater redemption and restoration of both Israel and the rest of the world, at the final coming of Messiah.

How This Study Guide Is Organized

The book of Isaiah, like any other biblical work, can be examined in different ways. However, what seems most logical (and perhaps easiest to track) is the sequential method we have used in other study guides in this series. All we really have to do, once we've identified the parts, is to recognize where one part ends and the next one begins.

At the same time, we will deal in greater detail with the major themes of Isaiah, identified above, as they emerge from the text of the book itself. To accomplish all of that, we have organized this study guide into ten text-linked chapters, plus a final summary. As shown in the table of contents, each of the first ten chapters in this guide deals with a "cluster" of chapters from Isaiah. Some of these groupings are larger than others, but for the most part they are reasonably consistent in size. More important, we have tried to organize the groupings to show how Isaiah dealt with a series of different topics, each one related to an overall theme.

In that sense, each of our chapters is topical in nature but sequential in how it examines the basic material. And if that doesn't make sense to you at this point, don't worry! All these things will become clearer as we move forward.

At the same time, please be aware that the book of Isaiah does contain a number of references to places, people, and events that are sometimes metaphorical in nature—meaning that some known thing "stands in" for something else. Or some of those references seem straightforward but use names that are simply not familiar to the average reader. Indeed, some are obscure even to experienced Bible scholars.

For that reason we advise you to keep a good Bible dictionary handy so you can look up these words as you encounter them. This is good advice for the study of any portion of the Bible, but it is especially important to have such a resource available when you encounter unfamiliar words in a book such as Isaiah, which frequently uses what, in his day, were "local" or "topical" references. We will mention some of them and will sometimes provide brief explanations, but it simply is not possible for a study guide of this size to do a thorough job of defining all unfamiliar words and metaphorical references.

Finally, it's also worth mentioning that, like any other ancient Hebrew thinker, Isaiah sometimes seems to "go sideways" a bit to people like ourselves, raised with a slightly different Western mind-set. But given the tremendous range of Isaiah's material—some of it focused on individual people of his time, some of it focused on the cities and nations of his time, yet much of it focused on a far more distant time that was yet to come—the degree to which that material arranges itself naturally into different subjects and segments seems all the more remarkable.

But that shouldn't be surprising, for Isaiah was a remarkable man serving a God for whom the word *remarkable* doesn't even begin to suffice.

INDICTED IN THE COURTROOM OF GOD

ISAIAH 1:1–6:13

Before We Begin . . .

Do you have any favorite quotations from the book of Isaiah, not already mentioned in the introduction? If so, please list them below.

What do you think Isaiah's "commission" from God was all about? What was he specifically called to do?

No one would ever accuse the prophet Isaiah of "modernism" in any form whatsoever. Neither would anyone suggest that he might be called a "modern thinker." After all, Isaiah was an ancient prophet of God, a man who devoted his entire life to telling people things they didn't want to hear—about themselves, about their actions, and most of all about the consequences of what they were doing.

That is what often comes to mind when we think about Isaiah, perhaps the best-known of the Hebrew prophets. And yet Isaiah begins his book with a remarkably clear statement that instantly answers four of the famous five "W questions" of modern journalism. Once again, here is the opening verse, and here is how those answers lay out:

The vision of Isaiah the son of Amoz, which he saw concerning Judah and Jerusalem in the days of Uzziah, Jotham, Ahaz, and Hezekiah, kings of Judah. (Isa. 1:1 NKJV)

Who?—The "who" is Isaiah, the son of Amoz, which was about as clear an identification as you could make in eighth-century BC Hebrew society.

What?—The "what" is the vision given to him by God.

Where?—The "where" is Jerusalem.

When?—The "when" is during the reigns of four well-known kings of Judah, the first of which began in 790 BC and the last of which ended in 686 BC (although Isaiah was clearly still around in 681 BC—see the introduction).

Why?—This is the only question Isaiah does not specifically answer in the first verse. But his work itself provides its own explanation. He wrote the book because God gave him a specific message to relate.

On the other hand, it's not likely that Isaiah really believed that his words would change the course of what was then contemporary history. Nonetheless he probably had two basic reasons for writing them down—first, to put them in front of as many people as he could while they were still fresh and while they might still have current application; and second, to pass on the words of God to future generations, that we might be aware of how loving and fair God has always been with His people, even when their actions required stern parental discipline.

In that sense, the book of Isaiah serves as both a historical record and a warning to future generations. And also, of course, it provides the entire world with additional, irrefutable proof that the God who created the universe and exists "outside of time" knows—even now—what will happen hundreds of years into the future.

However, in one sense, much of the "vision" Isaiah referred to in his first verse literally did come true during his lifetime. Most of what he wrote was directed toward Judah, the Southern Kingdom, for this was where he lived and these were the people he was most familiar with. But Israel, the Northern Kingdom, was captured by Assyria in 722 BC, just as Judah would be captured by Babylonia fewer than 140 years later.

THE LORD'S LAWSUIT AGAINST THE NATION (1:2–31)

In his first chapter, Isaiah essentially "lays out God's case" against the children of Israel. He follows a simple format. First, in verse 2, speaking on the Lord's behalf, he appeals to the heavens and the earth to "hear and give ear" to what he is about to say about God's children. Those children have rebelled against the Lord even though He nourished them and brought them up.

In verse 3, Isaiah compares Israel unfavorably to two animals. Unlike Israel, which animal knows its owner?

Unlike Israel again, which animal knows its master's crib?

Isaiah then lists a series of consequences, all phrased in the present tense as though they were happening "in the moment." Here is how this particular series is organized in verses 4–7:

First, Isaiah calls Israel a sinful nation; "a people laden with iniquity, a brood of evildoers."

Then he recounts some of the specifics—they have "forsaken the LORD," provoked Him to anger, and turned away from Him.

Next, Isaiah begins to list some of the consequences of the above; for example, Israel will be sick "from the sole of the foot even to the head."

Can you name three additional consequences that Isaiah lists in verse 7?

In verses 8–10, Isaiah continues his list of comparisons, now likening Israel to the ultimate cities of sin and corruption. Those two cities are:

Isaiah follows, in verses 11–15, with a list of the ways in which God was no longer willing to accept the self-righteous, hypocritical offerings that Israel still tried to make. Name three things that God said He had had enough of, or that He no longer delighted in:

In verses 16–20, as God had so often done down through the centuries, He once again (via the words of Isaiah) comforted His people and told them how to undo much of what they'd done. "Make yourselves clean," He said; "Put away the evil of your doings before my eyes" (v. 16).

Fill in, below, the remainder of verse 18, which begins, "Come now, and let us reason together . . ."

This is truly the voice of a God of infinite patience, love, and understanding. Isaiah then concludes chapter 1 with two segments—first a lament, in verses 21–23, and then another warning of judgment in verses 24–31.

What has befallen the "faithful city" (Israel/Judah) according to verses 21–23?

1.

2.

3.

What will happen to Israel, according to verses 24–31, if things continue as they have been?

1.

2.

3.

4.

SOWING AND REAPING (2:1–4:6)

Isaiah begins chapter 2 with a dramatic shift, from an indictment of Judah for her sin to a long section, spanning two complete chapters, in which he does four things:

First, in verses 1–4 Isaiah reaffirms Jerusalem's eventual position as the spiritual capital of the world, which is what it would become in the one thousand years of peace (i.e., the millennial kingdom) that would follow Christ's return to earth.

For example, complete these familiar lines from Isaiah 2:4 (NKJV):

> *They shall beat their swords into _____,*
> *And their spears into _____ _____;*
> *Nation shall not lift up _____ against nation,*
> *Neither shall they learn _____ anymore.*

Second, in verses 6–11, Isaiah again described Judah's current condition.

To get a sense of these verses, fill in the blanks below:

Their land is also full of _____;
They _____ the work of their own hands.
(Isa. 2:8 NKJV)

Third, in chapters 2:12–4:1, Isaiah describes the consequences that would follow in the meantime if Judah continued on her present course. The individual comments are too varied and numerous to list here, but the overall thrust is clear. Read these verses carefully for the rich imagery and vivid descriptions Isaiah includes. In the eyes of your imagination, you can almost see the finery that the Lord will take away in that day:

. . . the jingling anklets, the scarves, and the crescents; the pendants, the bracelets, and the veils; the headdresses, the leg ornaments, and the headbands; the perfume boxes, the charms, and the rings; the nose jewels, the festal apparel, and the mantles; the outer garments, the purses, and the mirrors; the fine linen, the turbans, and the robes. (Isa. 3:18–23 NKJV)

This description sounds amazingly modern in many ways! And who says we are now any more "beautifully adorned" than the ancients, anyway?

Fourth, in 4:2–6, Isaiah gives us a lovely description of the way things would be for Israel in the distant future. What is most striking here is the comparison of that yet-to-be time to the nation of Israel's own exodus from Egypt when, led by Moses, they followed a cloud by day and a pillar of fire by night.

In verse 6, Isaiah also refers to a tabernacle that would provide _____, a place of _____, and a shelter from _____ and _____.

WHAT IS THE "MILLENNIAL KINGDOM"?

The word *millennial* comes from the Latin word *mille*, meaning one thousand. Thus the millennial kingdom is the thousand-year reign of Christ on earth, which will begin when He returns to earth in the end times. It will end with the final judgment of all humanity, which leads into eternity for all, either with God or separated from God.

This is how the term will be used in this study guide. At best, however, the above is no more than a brief summary of what might be called the "mainline" Christian viewpoint of one major aspect of the end times. Other conceptual and theological variations exist—we urge the reader to refer to other sources for additional research.

A SONG BY ISAIAH (5:1–7)

In the first seven verses of chapter 5, Isaiah sings a song he composed himself, a song in which he again expresses God's love for His people, whom he clearly identifies in verse 7 as "the house of Israel." Nonetheless, he pulls no punches; especially poignant is verse 2, which, after describing the care God took in digging up the ground, clearing out the stones, and building a tower and a winepress, declares that the "grapes" God got in return for all His labor were not sweet and domestic but "wild" instead.

Isaiah then asks the reader, once again, to judge between God and His people, to see who had been faithful to whom. And the answer, of course, is beyond doubt, as expressed at the end of verse 7 (NKJV): "He looked for justice, but behold, oppression; for righteousness, but behold, a cry for help."

More Indictments (5:8–30)

In the next twenty-three verses, Isaiah mentions several more unpleasant results that would someday befall the people of Judah for their sin. He also pronounces a series of "woes" on specific people, or groups of people. Here are several examples; can you find the verses (all in chapter 5) in which these quotations appear?

1. *Woe to materialists ("those who join house to house").*
   Verse _____

2. *Woe to drunkards ("those who rise early . . . [to] follow intoxicating drink").*
   Verse _____

3. *Woe to the amoral ("those who call evil good").*
   Verse _____

4. *Woe to the vain and conceited ("those who are wise in their own eyes").*
   Verse _____

5. *Woe to peddlers and those who take bribes ("those who justify the wicked for a bribe").*
   Verse _____

Isaiah's Commission (Chapter 6)

This section of Isaiah ends with chapter 6, which presents several intriguing questions right off the top. Here are just three worth thinking about:

1. As we have mentioned in previous books in this study guide series, not all Hebrew writings were sequential in the modern sense. In other words, not all of the chapters and sec-

tions within the chapters are presented in chronological order. Chapter 6 could be one of those chapters, for even though Isaiah said previously that he prophesied during the reign of Uzziah, he now speaks about a vision that came to him in the year Uzziah died.

Does this seem like a sequencing problem to you, or would you interpret this in some other way?

2. In verse 1, Isaiah says that he "saw the Lord sitting on a throne, high and lifted up," with the train of His robe filling the temple. But even though God could take any form He wants, He would normally be invisible.

So who do you believe Isaiah saw? God the Father? Jesus Christ? Or a vision given to him by God that Isaiah could express only in terms that were familiar to him and his historical era?

"HIGH AND LIFTED UP"

As we make clear in several places in this study guide, the book of Isaiah has provided a wealth of quotations and catch phrases to both the religious and the secular world. This particular phrase is used as the title of at least one popular Christian worship song.

3. In the rest of this chapter, Isaiah provides a series of fascinating details about what he actually saw. Many of these are intriguing on several levels—read each verse carefully! Pay particular attention to verse 8, one of the more familiar quotations from Isaiah in which he literally volunteers to do the work of the Lord.

But verse 8, again, raises the question of sequence. Isaiah was already commissioned by God back in chapter 1. How do you, therefore, interpret this verse and the chapter that contains it—is it "out of order," or is it simply repeating a portion of Isaiah's original calling as a way of emphasizing something of huge importance to him—and to us as well?

PULLING IT ALL TOGETHER . . .

• Isaiah begins by recounting his commission, telling who he is, what he was called to do, where (and to whom) he ministered, and when he did it. Only the why aspect is not spelled out specifically . . . but this will emerge from Isaiah's own words as we study the rest of the book.

• Even in this short section (just six chapters), Isaiah speaks in a number of different voices and modes, from indictment and condemnation to comfort and assurance. Thus the sheer variety of his message is amazing all by itself.

• Also, like so much else of Isaiah, the first six chapters provide a number of memorable quotations, many of which have been part of "contemporary" language for hundreds of years.

2 | THE COMING MESSIAH

Before We Begin ...

In historical terms, two huge misfortunes (both quite similar, even "sym-metrical") befell the nation of Israel in Isaiah's time, one while he was alive and the other after he died. What were those misfortunes?

Why do you believe Isaiah would accept the commission God gave him, to take on the sometimes difficult duties of a prophet? What kind of man must he have been?

Chapters 7–12 of Isaiah include prophecies about the deliverance that God would provide for Judah/Israel. Though some of these prophecies were fulfilled fairly quickly, others are generally considered "messianic" in character, meaning that they pertain exclusively to Jesus Christ the Messiah, who was born to a virgin named Mary hundreds of years later in what is known as His First Coming.

Other prophecies made by Isaiah refer to events yet to come in the end times. These also involve Christ, the promised Messiah, coming for the final time to rule earth during the one-thousand-year millennial kingdom. This will occur prior to the final judgment of all men and women by God, at which time heaven and earth will pass away and the spirits of all will then be either with God for eternity in heaven or separated from Him for eternity in what is commonly called hell.

How Do You Define "Hell"?

Whether hell is a physical place of eternal fires and endless torment—as conceived by many—or something else entirely, is almost irrelevant. Being separated from God, and knowing that you could never come back into His presence and "take back" your denial of Him, would certainly be torment enough.

The only other alternative—that we pass, at death, into some kind of "endless nothingness" with no awareness whatsoever—is simply not supported in Scripture.

In particular, Isaiah 7:14 is usually considered one of the most striking references to the birth of Jesus Christ. Here is part of the text; please fill in the blanks below to reacquaint yourself with this ultra-familiar passage:

Behold, the _____ shall conceive and bear a _____, and shall call His name _____.
(Isa. 7:14 NKJV)

(Immanuel is only one of many names by which Isaiah refers to God the Father and God the Son.)

What's in a Name?

The original Hebrew text of the Bible contained a number of different references to God, the Creator of all. As transliterated into English, these include YHWH (or YHVH), Elohim, Adonai, and YHVH Tzva'ot. Each of these designations can be easily researched, and each one has a distinct meaning of its own.

Perhaps the most familiar is the four-letter designation YHWH, commonly translated as Yahweh, from which we get our English word *Jehovah*. Ironically, Hebrew has no *J* sound, so the very first letter of Jehovah simply cannot be authentic.

However, the prophet Isaiah also used a number of metaphorical references to God, including the previously mentioned "Holy One of Israel," which he employed twenty-six separate times.

The only problem some readers might have with these six chapters of Isaiah (i.e., 7–12) is in understanding what Isaiah was referring to at various points. So, as we will do several times in this study guide, let us deal with the organizational issue via the following outline, which breaks these chapters down into four parts. In each case, there is a very brief explanation of what Isaiah had to say, followed by questions on each of the chapters and verses themselves.

1. BIRTH OF THE MESSIAH (CHAPTER 7)

This chapter begins with a message from Isaiah to King Ahaz, one of the most evil of the kings of Judah. Ahaz refused Isaiah's invitation to ask for a sign from the Lord, but God gave him one anyway in verses 14–16. Though parts of this short passage have been interpreted in various ways, most scholars agree that they refer to the birth of the coming Messiah, Jesus Christ.

The remainder of chapter 7, beginning with verse 17, deals with King Ahaz and his experiences with the Assyrians, the details of which can be found in 2 Kings 15:38–16:20 and 2 Chronicles 27:9–28:27.

What was the name of Isaiah's son, as given in Isaiah 7:3?

What did King Ahaz refuse to do in Isaiah 7:12?

MESSIANIC REFERENCES IN ISAIAH

Isaiah contains a great wealth of messianic references. Brought together and considered as a whole in this fairly complete list, they give us a wealth of details that were revealed by God to Isaiah about the coming Messiah. Isaiah said that He would . . .

1. Be called before His birth to be God's Servant (49:1)
2. Be born of a virgin (7:14)
3. Be a descendant of Jesse, thus in the line of David (11:1, 10)
4. Be empowered by the Holy Spirit (11:2; 42:1)
5. Show gentleness toward the weak (42:3)
6. Obey the Lord in His mission (50:4–9)
7. Willingly submit to suffering (50:6; 53:7–8)
8. Be rejected by Israel (49:7; 53:1, 3)
9. Willingly take on the sin of the world (53:4–6, 10–12)
10. Triumph over death (53:10)
11. Be exalted (52:13; 53:12)
12. Be charged to comfort Israel and bring vengeance to the wicked (61:1–3)
13. Manifest God's glory (49:3)
14. Restore Israel spiritually to God (49:5) and to the land (49:8)
15. Reign on David's throne (9:7)
16. Bring joy to Israel (9:2)
17. Make a new covenant with Israel (42:6; 49:8–9)
18. Be a light to the Gentiles (42:6; 49:6)
19. Restore the nations (11:10)
20. Be worshiped by Gentiles (49:7; 52:15)
21. Govern the world (9:6)
22. Judge in righteousness, justice, and faithfulness (11:3-5; 42:1, 4)

In Isaiah 7:23, Isaiah says that a place in the land of Judah that could support a thousand vines for growing grapes would support something else instead. What would that "something else" be?

2. THE COMING DELIVERER (8:1–9:7)

This section deals with the same subject as the previous section—troubles between the Northern and Southern Kingdoms and the coming Assyrian invasion that would first swallow up the Northern Kingdom, then affect the Southern Kingdom too. But Judah (i.e., the Southern Kingdom) would be delivered from Assyria. Then, in chapter 9:1–7, Isaiah again describes the ultimate Deliverer who would one day deliver from their sin all the people of the world who were willing to accept His offer.

In Isaiah 8:3, Isaiah says he "went to the prophetess" (i.e., his wife—see "Can a Woman Be a Prophet Too?" on page 26) and she bore a son. What name does God instruct Isaiah to give to his second son?

In Isaiah 8:5–6, the king of Assyria is compared to something that would overflow and pass through the land of Judah, thus conquering and destroying the Northern Kingdom. What does God, speaking through Isaiah, compare the king of Assyria to?

CAN A WOMAN BE A PROPHET TOO?

All of the Old Testament prophets who have books named after them are men. But does this mean that only men could be prophets in ancient times? The Old Testament mentions several exceptions, but three obvious ones should be enough to answer the question.

The first exception would be Miriam, the sister of Moses, who is called a prophetess in Exodus 15:20, the verse that introduces the well-known "Song of Miriam" that she sang after the children of Israel passed through the Red Sea. The second exception would be Deborah, whose notable role in Israel's history is mentioned in Judges 4, beginning with verse 4. The third exception would be a woman named Noadiah, who is mentioned together with Tobiah and Sanballat in Nehemiah 6:14 as one who opposed Nehemiah's work in rebuilding the wall of Jerusalem. Which proves (as Balaam and his talking donkey also demonstrated!) that not all prophets worked for the Lord.

In Isaiah 8:13, who does the Lord tell Isaiah he should hallow, fear, and dread?

Isaiah 8:14 says that this same person will be a sanctuary to Isaiah, but what will He be to both houses of Israel?

Here is the text of Isaiah 8:19 (NKJV). Fill in the empty blanks:

And when they say to you, "Seek those who are mediums and wizards, who whisper and mutter," should not a people seek their God? Should they seek the _____ on behalf of the _____?

Who does God mean when He refers to "the dead"?

When Isaiah speaks of "the land of _____ and the land of _____" in Isaiah 9:1, what is "the land of" designation a metaphor for? And why would he use the two names mentioned above to refer to it? (For more information on this subject, see "Why 'Ephraim' for the Northern Kingdom?" on page 53 of this study guide.)

Fill in the blanks below for these two extremely well-known quotations from Isaiah 9:2 and 9:6 (NKJV):

The people who walked in _____ have seen a great _____.

For unto us a _____ is born, unto us a _____ is given; and the government will be upon His _____. And His name will be called _____, Counselor, Mighty God, Everlasting _____, Prince of _____.

3. EXILE FOR THE NORTHERN KINGDOM (9:8–10:4)

This section focuses on the fall of the Northern Kingdom to Assyria, which occurred in 722 BC.

In Isaiah 9:10, what is "fallen down"? What will it be rebuilt with?

In the same verse, what is "cut down"? What will it be replaced with?

In Isaiah 9:17, the Lord will have no joy in . . .

4. ASSYRIA'S FALL AND THE RISE OF THE FINAL KINGDOM (10:5–12:6)

In this section, Isaiah once again alternates his descriptions of soon-to-come events with distant events, and the transient fate of various kingdoms of earth with the eternal, triumphant nature of the kingdom of God. Chapter 10 speaks of what will befall the Assyrians, then of how the remnant of God's people will one day return to the land He gave them.

WHY "BRANCH" AND "STUMP"?

The words *branch* and *stump* represent just two out of literally dozens (hundreds?) of what we might call "agricultural references" in the Bible. The reason these occur is no mystery, but it is something some readers of the Bible do not think about. God's Word is written in what we would now call the "common vernacular" of the times in which its authors lived. They lived close to the earth and close to all the natural processes of raising sheep and cattle and growing crops for both food and clothing. Their frequent references to growing things, to seasons, to vineyards, to winepresses, and to fig trees were as natural as breathing (and even more natural, perhaps, than references to hard drives and processor speeds would be to computer users today!). Thus, to speak of a branch (David) coming from a stump (Jesse) would be—truly—to speak the language of the times.

Chapter 11 then continues with one of the greatest prophecies of the Bible, about a "Rod" and a "Branch" coming up from the stump of Jesse, who was David's father. Clearly, this passage refers to Christ, the Messiah, who was born "of the house of David."

A few verses later, Isaiah again speaks of a return to the land of Israel, only this time he is talking about what will happen just prior to the beginning of the millennial kingdom in the end times, when the true citizens of the true nation of Israel will be gathered from the entire world and brought back to their homeland. Here are Isaiah's inspiring words:

> It shall come to pass in that day
> That the LORD shall set His hand again the second time
> To recover the remnant of His people who are left,
> From Assyria and Egypt,
> From Pathros and Cush,
> From Elam and Shinar,
> From Hamath and the islands of the sea.
>
> He will set up a banner for the nations,
> And will assemble the outcasts of Israel,
> And gather together the dispersed of Judah
> From the four corners of the earth.
> Also the envy of Ephraim shall depart,
> And the adversaries of Judah shall be cut off;
> Ephraim shall not envy Judah,
> And Judah shall not harass Ephraim.
> (Isa. 11:11–13 NKJV)

Here, "Ephraim" refers to the Northern Kingdom, while "Judah" refers to the Southern Kingdom. In other words, there shall be no more division of the nation of Israel into separate parts.

Chapter 12, the final chapter in this section of Isaiah, containing only six verses, is a hymn of praise reflecting back on chapter 11. It speaks of the time ("in that day") when the true and complete nation of Israel will be finally restored to the land of Israel—at the start of the millennial kingdom.

PULLING IT ALL TOGETHER . . .

• This section of the book of Isaiah includes some clear references to the coming Messiah.

• It also predicts the fall of the Northern Kingdom of Israel, which happened a few years later.

• Toward the end of this section, Isaiah prophesies about the fall of Assyria, then segues into a discussion of what will happen during the end times.

3   JUDGMENT TIME

ISAIAH 13:1–23:18

Before We Begin . . .

In Isaiah 20:2–6, God commands Isaiah to remove his outer garment of sackcloth and his sandals, and thus to go naked (but not completely naked— he still wore an undergarment). God also commanded other prophets to do things we might call "strange" or even "unreasonable" by our standards. If you had Isaiah's relationship with God and had been given comparable responsibilities, how do you think you might respond in the same situation?

Some scholars consider these eleven chapters to be among Isaiah's more controversial ones, at least in terms of verification. They represent a clear and obvious departure from most of what Isaiah wrote up to this point, although he does repeat some of the same themes featured in earlier chapters.

Essentially, these chapters break down into nine separate prophecies about the coming fate of nine of the cities or countries in the area surrounding the nation of Israel. They also include one prophecy about the "wilderness" or "desert" itself (chapter 21), which could be a city, and one more about Jerusalem (chapter 22). Perhaps a bit of history will help put these chapters in perspective.

Sennacherib was the king of Assyria from 705 BC until his death in 681 BC. Under him, the Assyrian empire was destined to

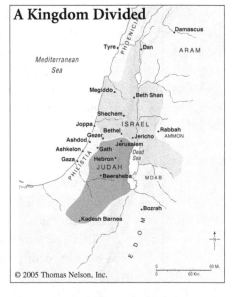

A Kingdom Divided

© 2005 Thomas Nelson, Inc.

bring about a tremendous amount of devastation throughout the entire area, including the sacking of Babylon in 689 BC. But prior to all that, his father was a man named Sargon, who built a large empire that Sennacherib inherited, stretching from the Persian Gulf in the southeast to the middle of Asia Minor in the northwest, well beyond the Mediterranean Sea and halfway to the Black Sea. Present-day Iraq (including Babylon), Syria, much of central Turkey, and a good-sized chunk of Iran were included.

When Sennacherib came to power, the challenge he faced was twofold. First, he had to try to hold on to all the hostile territory that his father had already at least partially conquered. Second, he wanted to add to it by conquering other lands and cities as well, including both the Northern and Southern Kingdoms of Israel.

Sennacherib's campaign against Jerusalem, with Isaiah (in his role as prophet and counselor) mentioned several times, is told in 2 Kings 18 and 19. Against Isaiah's advice, King Hezekiah of Judah formed an alliance with Phoenicia and Philistia, which was also supposed to include some support from Egypt. But instead of depending on these near-worthless allies, Hezekiah eventually rescued himself and his kingdom by following Isaiah's advice and turning the whole Sennacherib-at-the-gates scenario over to God. This resulted in the nocturnal angel-of-God death of 185,000 of Sennacherib's troops without the loss of a single Israelite, and sent the surviving Assyrians on a fast (and doubtless confused and unhappy!) march back to Ninevah. Thus Jerusalem was saved, literally by the hand of God, if only for a few more years.

Despite what we do know about these times, part of the difficulty in assessing the accuracy of Isaiah's prophecies against the cities is the lack of contemporary, extrabiblical evidence to fill in and confirm all the details. Although Isaiah was speaking of specific cities and nations of his era, he was also looking beyond his own times and providing a metaphorical picture of the even greater devastation to come in the end times. In fact, his message was probably directed as much (or more) to future generations, certainly not exclusively to those of his own time, most of whom probably never heard or read it anyway.

With all that in mind, let us briefly review, in order, each of Isaiah's separate yet interrelated prophecies from this section of his book. To aid in sorting out the material, questions are included to help you work through each section.

BABYLON (13:1–14:27)

The first verse of this section is sometimes cited as proof that Isaiah truly was capable of prophesying about future events, for it identifies him, unmistakably, as the "son of Amoz" and thus leaves no doubt about his identity—or about what would happen to Babylon at a then-future time. Babylon, for its part, clearly deserved God's wrath. From its very first days, it had been associated with anti-God apostasy of every kind, including outright rebellion, idol worship, and even the invention of astrology and its related (yet decidedly pagan) "signs."

WHAT DO WE MEAN BY "ORACLE"?

In the Bible, the word *oracle* is often used to identify both a messenger and a message from God. It was used in ancient Greek times for the priests and priestesses of various pagan gods, but in the Bible it is reserved almost exclusively for men like Isaiah and Jeremiah, for the messages that God brought to the world through their writings. Interestingly, though the word appears in several other prophetic books (including Jeremiah and Hosea), it does not appear even once in the book of Isaiah—at least not in the New King James Version. Nonetheless, it is an appropriate word to use in connection with some of Isaiah's proclamations.

The remaining verses of this section constitute a "proclamation" or an "oracle" against Babylon. Most striking to many readers, however, is the inclusion of the name Lucifer in Isaiah 14:12. Many people have interpreted this as a reference to Satan, from which they then derive the name Lucifer and attach it to the devil himself. On the contrary, most Bible scholars agree that verse 14 actually refers to Sennacherib, who was certainly a man of some evil but definitely not on Satan's level.

WHO WAS THIS GUY CALLED "LUCIFER"?

As indicated elsewhere, many people believe that "Lucifer" in Isaiah 14:12 is a direct reference to Satan (which, in turn, comes from *Ha'Satan*, his title in Hebrew) and that Lucifer was even a common name for the devil in Isaiah's time. But the word *lucifer* itself comes from a fourth-century AD Latin translation of this verse—*quomodo cecidisti de caelo **lucifer** qui mane oriebaris corruisti in terram qui vulnerabas gentes* (emphasis added)—which eventually found its way into most English translations. In the Latin translation, the word *Lucifer* was simply another name for Venus—the "morning star" Venus. The Latin word, in turn, came from another word meaning "bright light" or "to shine brightly."

In other words, Lucifer has gradually become a common name for Satan, but this is probably not how Isaiah meant it at all. On the contrary, he was referring to Sennacherib, the "rising star" of the then-near future who would eventually be eclipsed—just as all earthly conquerors eventually are.

In Isaiah 13:11, why does God say He will punish the world?

Why will He punish the wicked?

Fill in the blanks for the remainder of verse 11 (NKJV):

> *I will halt the _____ of the proud,*
> *And will lay low the haughtiness of the _____.*

To whom is Isaiah referring in the following passage?

> *For you have said in your heart: "I will ascend into heaven, I will exalt my throne above the stars of God; I will also sit on the mount of the congregation on the farthest sides of the north; I will ascend above the heights of the clouds, I will be like the Most High." (Isa. 14:13–14 NKJV)*

PHILISTIA (14:28–32)

The reference to "the rod that struck you" in verse 29 of this oracle against the province of Philistia was not King Ahaz—as some might think—but was probably Assyria. In 711 BC, some four years after Isaiah wrote these verses, Assyria defeated the city of Ashdod and put all of Philistia under Assyrian rule. This particular conquest, incidentally, was not the work of Sennacherib but of his father, Sargon, both of whom are referenced above.

MOAB (CHAPTERS 15–16)

By the time of Isaiah, the nation of Israel had a long history of conflict with the country known as Moab in biblical times. The word "Moab" occurs 165 times in the New King James Version of the Bible, and many of those times it means trouble of one kind or another for Israel. That "trouble" ranges from the marriage of numerous Israelite men to Moabite women (and thus the repeated introduction into Israel of pagan, idolatrous influences) to direct military action, as in the cases of both Saul and David.

WAS EVERYTHING FROM MOAB BAD NEWS?

Not necessarily! The notable exception, of course, is the woman known as Ruth, who came from Moab but became what some consider the quintessential "grafted-in" Israelite. Through her union with Boaz, which produced Obed, who then had a son named Jesse, Ruth eventually became—literally—the great-grandmother of David. Thus she was also a direct ancestor of Christ Himself.

These two chapters begin with the defeat of Moab (and the flight of her surviving people southward into Edom), detail God's concurrent protection of Israel, add a six-verse dissertation by Isaiah on Moab's pride and conceit, and end with two verses prophesying her destruction within three years.

Here are some short extracts from chapter 16. To get a good sense of how this section reads, fill in the blanks below:

Verse 6: We have heard of the pride of Moab—he is very _____.

Verse 7: Therefore Moab shall wail for Moab; _____ shall wail.

Verse 9: Therefore I will _____ the vine of Sibmah, with the weeping of Jazer; I will drench you with my tears, O Heshbon and Elealeh.

Verse 11: Therefore my _____ shall resound like a _____ for Moab.

Damascus (17:1–11) and the Land of Whirring Wings (17:12–18:7)

Both of these oracles are of a similar nature, differing only in the details and the language Isaiah used. Damascus, of course, was the ancient city that retained its name into modern times. Then it was situated in a land called Aram; now that same land is known as Syria.

Likewise, the "land of buzzing wings" (which some scholars consider a reference to frequent locust infestations) was the land then called Cush but now known as Ethiopia.

Read the following passage and answer the questions that follow:

For before the harvest, when the bud is perfect
And the sour grape is ripening in the flower,
He will both cut off the sprigs with pruning hooks
And take away and cut down the branches.
(Isa. 18:5 NKJV)

In the above passage, who is the "He" of whom Isaiah speaks?

What authority does that person have?

What is the metaphor he is using?

What industry or occupation do the metaphors in Isaiah often relate to? Why would this be so?

Why did the speaker so frequently use metaphors of this general type?

EGYPT (CHAPTERS 19–20)

Isaiah makes it clear in chapters 19–20 that Egypt will be no help at all to any of the other nations of the region that might be looking for support against the impending doom from Assyria. Like the other nations in Assyria's path, Egypt also will be punished by God, as detailed in Isaiah 19. Chapter 20 deals with the conquest of both Egypt and Cush.

In chapter 19, Isaiah also amplifies three reasons why Egypt would not be in a position to help any others. First, Egypt had a number of internal problems, within both the people running the country and the systems they'd put in place, that would lead to uncertainty, disorganization, and despair. Second, a drought would bring Egypt to her knees, for this time she would not have Joseph, acting at the Lord's behest (as he did in Genesis), to supervise preparations during the bountiful seasons and manage Egypt's reserves during the scarce times. Third, as He did before the Exodus in Moses' time, God would demonstrate that all of Egypt's mystics and "wise" men would be as fools before the infinite wisdom of the Lord.

Isaiah 19:5 (NKJV) says: "The waters will fail from the sea, and the river will be wasted and dried up." What river, and what sea, is this verse talking about?

Isaiah 19:6–7 (NKJV) says: "The reeds and rushes will wither. The papyrus reeds by the River, . . . and everything sown by the River, will wither, be driven away, and be no more." If this had happened centuries earlier, while the Israelites were still enslaved in Egypt, what great patriarch would have had to come into the world in a "different" way—and why?

THE "WILDERNESS OF THE SEA" (21:1–10), EDOM (21:11–12), AND ARABIA (21:13–17)

Chapter 21 includes three relatively brief oracles. The first is against what Isaiah calls "the Wilderness of the Sea" in the New King James Version, and "the Desert by the Sea" in other translations. There are two differing interpretations of what this designation means.

The first interpretation is that the "Wilderness of the Sea" (21:1) refers to Babylon and that this passage predicts the fall of Babylon to the Medo-Persians in 539 BC.

The second interpretation is that the same designation (and/or its counterpart, "the Desert by the Sea") refers to the land area surrounding the northern curve of what we now know as the Persian Gulf and extending almost up to Babylon itself. This would correspond to the southeastern portion of the Assyrian empire largely built by Sargon and inherited by his son, to be defended and expanded if Sennacherib was able. But both Sargon and Sennacherib (and Babylon too!) had significant troubles with a Chaldean prince called Merodach Baladan, also mentioned in Isaiah 39:1. Sennacherib was finally able to subdue him, once and for all, by ravaging his home stomping grounds around the Persian Gulf in 702 BC.

Evidence for version one includes the names Elam and Media in Isaiah 21:2, which some interpreters put together with Babylon and assume the reference can only be to the fall of Babylon to the Medo-Persians. Evidence for version two is that Isaiah makes it clear that the vision he saw was a distressing development for Israel. Conversely, the eventual fall of Babylon in 539 BC was good news for Israel, because it led to their eventual return to their homeland. Also working in favor of version two is that Babylon has already been discussed, separately, in chapters 13 and 14.

(Incidentally, you need not choose an interpretation here—sometimes it's enough to know that different possibilities exist.)

The middle and last sections of Isaiah 21 deal with Edom and Arabia. In verse 11, the reference to Seir is to Edom (see Joshua 24:4, in which God reminded the Israelites that He'd given the mountains of Seir to Esau, whose descendants became the Edomites). The reference to Dumah is considered either a wordplay on Edom or a corruption of an ancient designation for Edom, by which it was known as Udumu or Idumea.

In the verses dealing with Arabia, "Dedanites" (21:13) refers to a tribe from southern Arabia, while Tema and Kedar were an oasis and a town in northern Arabia, respectively.

WHO WERE THE EDOMITES?

Edom, which was the name given to Esau when he sold his birthright to Jacob, means red, which also described the general hue of Esau's skin (and possibly his hair as well). Edom also became the name of the country God gave to Esau to separate him from his brother; his descendants were called Edomites. Edom was also called Mount Seir and Idumea, and several variations of the latter. It was a long, narrow, mountainous country extending southward from below the southern end of the Dead Sea, with its ancient capital at Bozrah.

Perhaps the most striking thing about the Edomites was the way in which Esau's descendants seemed to keep alive his bitter hatred for Jacob, even though this same hatred seemed to be somewhat abated when Jacob returned to the land of his birth after marrying Leah and Rachel. Many years later, the Edomites refused to let the Israelites, coming back from Egypt, pass through their land. Thereafter they continued to oppose the Israelites at various times, even attempting to invade Israel during the reign of Jehoshaphat in the tenth century BC.

JERUSALEM (CHAPTER 22)

The proclamation against Jerusalem that occupies all of Isaiah 22 is fairly straightforward. But it also includes a section, beginning with verse 15, that speaks against a steward named Shebna. Shebna seems to have been an official in the Jerusalem government who might have tried to negotiate in some "improper" way with Sennacherib (or one of his lieutenants), perhaps for a lofty grave or "sepulcher on high" (v. 16) that might guarantee himself a name for posterity.

When Isaiah says in 22:3 that "all your rulers have fled" and "are captured by the archers," what does he mean? Why would archers be more likely than swordsmen to capture someone who fled from a battle?

In 22:12, Isaiah says that God called for four different responses. What were they?

But instead, what was the response of the people Isaiah was addressing? Along with feeling "joy and gladness" at the wrong time, they did what four things?

1.

2.

3.

4.

What famous remark, repeated countless times in the centuries since it was written down, does Isaiah include in verse 13?

TYRE (CHAPTER 23)

The city of Tyre was founded close to two thousand years before Isaiah's time—perhaps as early as 2700 BC. Along with the city of Sidon, it was one of the Phoenician empire's richest port cities, located on the western shores of the Mediterranean Sea in what is now Lebanon. Tarshish, not too far away, could well have been the ancient city of Tartessus in southwest Spain, which most likely would have had a lucrative trading relationship with both Tyre and Sidon—and hence would "wail" at any calamity affecting Tyre.

Isaiah's proclamation against Tyre details what would eventually happen to the city. Although it was not completely destroyed until some two hundred years after Isaiah wrote these words, its trade was cut off sometime between 700 and 630 BC.

PULLING IT ALL TOGETHER . . .

• These chapters include eleven different prophecies, or "oracles," against eleven different entities.

• These entities were all cities or countries of Isaiah's time.

• Because we lack sufficient details about the history of the times in question, not every one of these prophecies can be proven true in every particular. But history does prove most of them correct in every way.

4   JUDGMENTS AND BLESSINGS

ISAIAH 24:1–27:13

Before We Begin . . .

This section of the book of Isaiah contains two chapters (25 and 26) of praise to God, both structured by Isaiah as songs to be sung, literally. How does this image of Isaiah, as a songwriter, match up with what you have learned about him to this point? Do the songs seem contradictory? Why, or why not?

In these four chapters, Isaiah changes his focus dramatically from the here-and-almost-now of the previous eleven proclamations. He concentrates instead on a distant time when the entire world would be under judgment for what—by then—would be far more sins than were part of the world's history in Isaiah's time. (If you doubt that, ask any old-timer to tell you how much worse the world has become since he or she was a child!)

This is, perhaps, one of the most straightforward and uncomplicated sections of the book of Isaiah. Often known as Isaiah's Apocalypse, these four chapters break down into two major sections—one chapter of judgment followed by three chapters detailing the blessings that would follow. Let us review, very briefly, each of the two sections, with a series of questions included to help you sort out the material each chapter contains.

JUDGMENTS (CHAPTER 24)

The opening of this chapter tells us that all people in the coming judgment will be treated equally. No hierarchy and no escaping for anyone—social rank, monetary wealth, corporate and/or professional positions, political affiliations, and all other forms of earthly status will be completely irrelevant.

Fill in the blanks below to see the comparisons Isaiah makes, in the language of his day.

> *And it shall be:*
> *As with the people, so with the _____;*
> *As with the servant, so with his _____;*
> *As with the maid, so with her _____;*
> *As with the buyer, so with the _____;*
> *As with the lender, so with the _____;*
> *As with the creditor, so with the _____.*
> *(Isa. 24:2 NKJV)*

Verse 5 (NKJV) then tells us that "the earth is also defiled under its inhabitants, because they have transgressed the laws, changed the ordinance, broken the everlasting covenant." Do you think this has anything to do with environmentalism?

What is a more likely explanation for Isaiah's claim that the "earth is defiled"? In what ways?

What do these two lines from verse 13 (NKJV) represent?

> *When it shall be thus in the midst of the land among the*
>   *people,*
> *It shall be like the shaking of an olive tree.*

Isaiah ends the chapter with these words (fill in the blanks):

> *Then the moon will be _____*
> *And the sun _____;*
> *For the LORD of hosts will reign*
> *On Mount Zion and in _____*
> *And before His elders, gloriously.*
> *(Isa. 24:23 NKJV)*

BLESSINGS (CHAPTERS 25–27)

Chapter 25 of Isaiah is an extended psalm in praise of God for His deliverance of His people. In that sense it is not unlike one of the more familiar psalms of David. Isaiah speaks of a feast on the mountain of the Lord; of food of all kinds; and of the best of meats and the finest of wines.

What kind of people will glorify God (v. 3)?

The noise of whom will be reduced (v. 5)?

What does the word referenced above mean in the context of verse 5?

What Is "on the Lees"?

Some things never change! In chapter 25, verse 6, Isaiah speaks twice of the wine "lees:" "A feast of wines on the lees . . . of well-refined wines on the lees."

The "lees" are the solid remains of the grapes that fall to the bottom of the barrel (or whatever containers might have been used in ancient times) after fermentation has consumed all the sugar in the juice and produced a clear liquid. Many wine-makers of today (and presumably of earlier times as well) leave the wine "on the lees" for a period of additional time after it is otherwise fully developed to impart as much extra flavor as possible to the liquid itself. Some modern cooks, with access to fresh lees (if the word *fresh* can actually be applied here!), add them to bread mixtures for extra flavor (and no, eating the bread does not lead to intoxica-tion—any alcohol would be baked out).

Whether wine was sometimes left "on the lees" until the moment when it was actually drunk, in ancient times, is an open question—although Christ's own refer-ence to "new wine in old wineskins" would suggest otherwise. But either way, the point Isaiah was making is that "in that day" of blessings, the people of God will drink wine at its best moment, when it is fully developed and all the residue and impurities have settled to the bottom.

What will God destroy "on this mountain" (v. 7)?

What will be "brought down" (v. 11)?

Chapter 26 is a song written by Isaiah that will be sung by the people of God "in the land of Judah" (i.e., the millennial kingdom). It includes the following verses, with blanks to be filled in below:

*"Trust in the L*ORD *_____,*
For in YAH [i.e., a shortened form of Yahweh], the
    L*ORD, is everlasting strength.*
For He brings down those who dwell on high,
The lofty _____;
He lays it low,
He lays it low to the _____,
He brings it down to the dust.
The foot shall _____ it down—
The feet of the poor
And the steps of the needy."

The way of the just is _____;
O Most Upright,
You weigh the path of the just.
Yes, in the way of Your _____,
*O L*ORD, *we have waited for You;*
The desire of our soul is for Your _____
And for the remembrance of You.
With my soul I have desired You in the _____,
Yes, by my spirit within me I will seek You early;
For when Your _____ are in the earth,
The _____ of the world will learn righteousness.

Let grace be shown to the wicked,
Yet he will not learn _____;
In the land of uprightness he will deal _____,
*And will not behold the majesty of the L*ORD.
(Isa. 26:4–10 NKJV)

In typical back-and-forth fashion, Isaiah then ends this chapter with a two-verse warning to the people of God, harkening back to the preceding "judgment" chapter, to "enter their chambers" and "shut their doors behind them" to avoid the judgment that will precede the blessings detailed previously.

Chapter 27 concludes this section of Isaiah and deals with salvation for God's people. It can be broken down into three sections of its own, beginning with the familiar words "in that day" in verses 1, 2, and 12 (although the phrase is then repeated in verse 13).

What does the Lord say He would "go through" in verse 4?

How would you interpret the following verse?

> *Has He struck Israel as He struck those who struck him?*
> *Or has He been slain according to the slaughter of those*
> *who were slain by Him? (Isa. 27:7 NKJV)*

What will be blown in verse 13? What do you believe this instrument will actually be?

PULLING IT ALL TOGETHER . . .

• In some ways, these four chapters can be among the easiest to follow, since most of the references are to things easily understood—or easily researched, if necessary.

• Even so, Isaiah does not follow what we might call a "modern" organizational scheme, alternating judgment with blessings and even inserting a clear warning into the first "blessings" chapter.

5

WOE UNTO YOU

ISAIAH 28:1–33:24

Before We Begin ...

Isaiah spoke both judgments and woes against the people of his day, including both the people of Israel and their enemies. What do you think would be the logical difference between a judgment and a woe?

When Isaiah characterized his messages from God as judgments or woes, from whose perspective do you think he was operating?

These six chapters of Isaiah continue in the most recent pattern, with two main differences.

First, Isaiah directs these five messages against the Israelites themselves, but more specifically against the leaders of both the Northern (Israel) and Southern (Judah) Kingdoms. Those leaders had two major failings:

1. They failed to pay attention to God's Word—a passive sin that we might call one of omission, but which can also be one of willful disobedience.

2. They sought out alliances with other nations, especially Egypt, to protect themselves against the Assyrians and other enemies—an active sin that we might call one of commission, but also a passive sin because they failed to trust in the Lord's ability and desire to protect them Himself.

Second, Isaiah calls these five messages woes rather than judgments. The distinction could almost be irrelevant, for they sound very much like God's judgments against Israel's enemies. However, they do tend to contain more displays of tenderness (from both God and Isaiah, perhaps) toward His own people, mixed in with the pronouncements of impending judgment.

As He had done since His first dealings with Adam, God revealed Himself as the divine Father who knows that He must discipline His children—but would rather not.

WOE TO EPHRAIM AND JUDAH—OR JERUSALEM (CHAPTER 28)

The words *Ephraim* and *Judah* refers to the Northern and Southern Kingdoms of Israel, respectively. The woes of this chapter are almost evenly divided between the two kingdoms, starting with the North (vv. 1–13) and moving to the South (vv. 14–29).

Many biblical scholars teach that the second half of the chapter, starting with its reference to Jerusalem in verse 14, actually refers to the city of Jerusalem exclusively (as reflected in the heading above), but others believe that the name Jerusalem is used in place of Judah only because of its status—and focus—as Judah's preeminent city. By this time Jerusalem was no longer the acknowledged capital of all Israel, but it had once been and still was Israel's greatest city. Also, as you will see, verses 24–28 in particular refer to plowing, sowing, threshing, and other crop-related activities better suited to the countryside than to the city.

esu WHY "EPHRAIM" FOR THE NORTHERN KINGDOM?

Ephraim and Manassah were the two sons of Joseph, who in turn was the next-to-last son of Jacob. By the middle of the eighth century BC (i.e., around 750 BC), after the nation of Israel split into the Northern and Southern Kingdoms, the tribe of Joseph had also split into two tribes, headed by his two sons. By approximately 745 BC, the tribe of Ephraim had become dominant among the northern tribes. For this reason, Isaiah and others sometimes called the Northern Kingdom "Ephraim," just as they called the Southern Kingdom "Judah" after the name of its own dominant tribe.

If you fill in the blanks in the verses below, you will see the distinction that the Lord, via the words of Isaiah, makes between the two kingdoms.

> *Woe to the crown of pride, to the drunkards of _____,*
> *Whose glorious beauty is a fading flower*
> *Which is at the head of the _____ _____,*
> *To those who are overcome with _____!*
> *(Isa. 28:1 NKJV)*

> *Therefore hear the word of the LORD, you scornful men,*
> *Who rule this people who are in _____,*
> *Because you have said, "We have made a _____*
>   *with death,*
> *And with Sheol we are in _____.*
> *When the overflowing scourge passes through,*
> *It will not come to us,*
> *For we have made _____ our refuge,*
> *And under _____ we have hidden ourselves."*
> *(Isa. 28:14–15 NKJV)*

What is your understanding of the word "Sheol" in the fourth line of the previous Scripture?

Do you think that the drunkenness mentioned in the first verse was a problem only in the north—or was it characteristic of both kingdoms?

THE PLACE OF THE DEAD

The Hebrew word *sheol* refers to the place of the dead; it's the place where people go when they die. In the Old Testament it was often used in a metaphorical way. A good example, besides the references in Isaiah, would be Psalm 49:14 (NASB), which says:

As sheep they are appointed for Sheol;
Death shall be their shepherd;
And the upright shall rule over them in the morning;
And their form shall be for Sheol to consume,
So that they have no habitation.

Another Hebrew word, *gehenna*, comes from *ge hinnom*, which refers to the Valley of Hinnom—the valley to the south of the temple in Jerusalem, where garbage was burned. Thus it was a place of perpetual fire. Both *sheol* and *gehenna*, in the Hebrew originals, were translated into English as "hell" in the King James Version—and thus they've been known ever since.

As you read this chapter and come to Isaiah 28:10, you will encounter a fascinating verse whose meaning can easily slip by. To understand what it probably represents, you have to back up to verses 7 and 8, in which Isaiah mentions the priests and prophets who were "swallowed up by wine" (there's a neat reverse metaphor!). In verse 9, Isaiah appears to have been including their answer to his many warnings, in which they responded to him by mocking him. Then, in verse 10, they mocked Isaiah even further by mimicking the way children are commonly taught—that is, by building "precept upon precept" (i.e., reinforcing the rules), teaching "here a little, there a little," and so on.

Whom will he teach knowledge?
And whom will he make to understand the message?
Those just weaned from milk?
Those just drawn from the breasts?
For precept must be upon precept, precept upon precept,
Line upon line, line upon line,
Here a little, there a little.
(Isa. 28:9–10 NKJV)

In the original Hebrew, verse 10 takes on even more of a mocking tone, for it includes a great deal of alliterative (i.e., similar-sounding) verbal constructions that do not transliterate into English. Also, the same words of mockery are repeated in verse 13.

WOE TO JERUSALEM (CHAPTER 29)

This chapter continues the woe directed toward the two kingdoms, except it now clearly concentrates on the city of Jerusalem itself (although, again, in practical terms it can be hard to separate the city from the kingdom). In the very first verse, the word *Ariel* is considered a direct reference to Jerusalem. The Hebrew word *Ariel* can also mean "lion of God" or "altar of burnt offerings," so this passage might be suggesting either that Jerusalem was a strong city with lion-like qualities or that it was the city in which the temple (with its altar) was located.

Consider just a few verses from this chapter, starting with . . .

> *It shall even be as when a hungry man dreams,*
> *And look—he eats;*
> *But he awakes, and his soul is still empty;*
> *Or as when a thirsty man dreams,*
> *And look—he drinks;*
> *But he awakes, and indeed he is faint,*
> *And his soul still craves:*
> *So the multitude of all the nations shall be,*
> *Who fight against Mount Zion.*
> *(Isa. 29:8 NKJV)*

What is the point of the above verse? What is Isaiah saying? (If you're not sure, read it again in context, and see if that helps.)

Next, fill in the blanks and notice the parallel thoughts:

> *The whole vision has become to you like the words of a*
> *_____ that is sealed, which men deliver to one*
> *who is _____, saying, "Read this, please."*

> *And he says, "I cannot, for it is sealed."*

> *Then the _____ is delivered to one who is*
> *_____, saying, "Read this, please."*

> *And he says, "I am not literate."*
> *(Isa. 29:11–12 NKJV)*

In that day the deaf shall hear the words of the

_____,

And the eyes of the _____ shall see out of

_____ and out of_____.

The _____ also shall increase their joy in the

  LORD,

And the poor among men shall _____

In the Holy One of Israel.

(Isa. 29:18–19 NKJV)

WOE TO THE OBSTINATE CHILDREN (CHAPTER 30)

The thirtieth chapter of Isaiah begins with the following two verses:

"Woe to the rebellious children," says the LORD,
"Who take counsel, but not of Me,
And who devise plans, but not of My Spirit,
That they may add sin to sin;
Who walk to go down to Egypt,
And have not asked My advice,
To strengthen themselves in the strength of Pharaoh,
And to trust in the shadow of Egypt!"
(Isa. 30:1–2 NKJV)

What does the Lord call the people of the nation of Israel in the first line of verse 1, above?

Why? What are they guilty of doing?

What does the Lord then call these same people in the first line of verse 9, below?

> *This is a rebellious people,*
> *Lying children,*
> *Children who will not hear the law of the LORD;*
> *Who say to the seers, "Do not see,"*
> *And to the prophets, "Do not prophesy to us right*
> *things;*
> *Speak to us smooth things, prophesy deceits."*
> *(Isa. 30:9–10 NKJV)*

What is the obvious parallel between this verse and the previous passage?

The remainder of this chapter is a woe against the folly of depending on an alliance with Egypt. It is continued in the next two chapters and will therefore be discussed in the next section. But meanwhile, here in chapter 30, Isaiah "goes sideways" again in verses 27–33, pronouncing a separate judgment on Assyria (which is not mentioned until verse 31), which Judah would soon defeat—as it turned out, in 701 BC.

WOE TO THE EGYPTIAN ALLIANCE (CHAPTERS 31–32)

Chapters 31 and 32 of Isaiah expand on what the prophet wrote in chapter 30. Based on the relatively clear way in which Isaiah laid out these two chapters, we have broken them down into five sections, or passages. Look at each passage separately, as detailed in the following list, then see if you can write a one-sentence summary of what each one is all about. What is the message God is delivering to the nation of Israel, through the words of Isaiah, in each of these passages? (Hint: If you are using the New King James Version, use the headings for each section as starting points.)

Isaiah 31:1–3

Isaiah 31:4–9

Isaiah 32:1–8

Isaiah 32:9–15

Isaiah 32:16–20

WOE TO DESTROYERS . . . AND DELIVERANCE FOR BELIEVERS (CHAPTER 33)

Chapter 33 of the book of Isaiah begins with a woe, then segues into what some commentators call a prayer, while others call it a proclamation. Either way, it has two parts, as we will see in a moment.

The first section of the chapter, which includes verses 1–12, talks about the woe that will come upon unbelievers who live without righteousness. Then comes the transition to the middle section, as shown in verses 12 and 13:

And the people shall be like the burnings of lime;
Like thorns cut up they shall be burned in the fire.
Hear, you who are afar off, what I have done;
And you who are near, acknowledge My might.
(Isa. 33:12–13 NKJV)

Who do you believe is the speaker in the passage above?

The middle section, which includes verses 13–16, talks about the people who will be saved. Fill in the blanks below to find out more about them.

He who walks _____ and speaks uprightly,
He who despises the gain of _____,
Who gestures with his hands, refusing _____,
Who stops his ears from hearing of _____,
And shuts his eyes from _____ evil.
(Isa. 33:15 NKJV)

Finally, verses 17–24 speak of the land in which those people will someday live.

Look upon _____, the city of our appointed
    feasts;
Your eyes will see _____, a quiet home,
A tabernacle that will not be taken down;
Not one of its stakes will ever be removed,
Nor will any of its cords be broken.
But there the majestic LORD will be for us
A place of broad _____ and _____,
In which no galley with oars will sail,
Nor majestic ships pass by.
(Isa. 33:20–21 NKJV)

What do you think Isaiah means when he speaks of "cords" and "stakes"?

PULLING IT ALL TOGETHER . . .

- The five woes contained within these chapters are quite similar in tone to the judgments that preceded them, except that they focus mainly on the Israelites and their futile attempts to protect and preserve themselves rather than trusting in God.

- Why Isaiah called them woes is not completely clear, although a judgment against his own people might involve more personal woe for Isaiah—and certainly for God Himself—than judgments against his (His) people's enemies.

- Jerusalem, the capital city of Judah/Israel, is included as one of the targets.

6   THE DAYS OF RECKONING

ISAIAH 34:1–35:10

Before We Begin . . .

Do you believe that a judgment can be a blessing? If so, can you think of any time in your own life when that was true?

Can a blessing also be a negative thing? Can you think of any examples of people whose lives were hindered by too many blessings?

Chapters 34 and 35 of Isaiah bring to a close a long series of indictments, judgments, and woes, interspersed with messages of deliverance and hope that, so far, have been very much in the minority. The tide begins to turn in the second of these two chapters, but not quite yet! First, we must deal with chapter 34.

THE LORD'S WRATH UPON THE NATIONS (CHAPTER 34)

Chapter 34 is only seventeen verses long, but it still divides into three parts. Verse 1 is an invitation to all nations and people to "hear and heed" what is about to come. The words that fit in these blanks tell us where those nations and people come from.

> *Come near, you nations, to hear;*
> *And heed, you people!*
> *Let the _____ hear, and all that is in it,*
> *The _____ and all things that come forth from it.*
> *(Isa. 34:1 NKJV)*

This short opening is followed by a three-verse statement of God's judgment against the armies of all the nations, whose dead bodies will one day rot in the sun.

For the _____ of the LORD is against all nations,
And His fury against all their armies;
He has utterly _____ them,
He has given them over to the _____.
Also their slain shall be thrown out;
Their _____ shall rise from their corpses,
And the _____ shall be melted with their blood.
All the host of heaven shall be dissolved,
And the heavens shall be rolled up like a _____;
All their host shall fall down
As the leaf falls from the _____,
And as fruit falling from a fig tree.
(Isa. 34:2–4 NKJV)

Finally, chapter 34 ends with a more specific judgment against Edom, which once again "stands in," like a metaphorical scapegoat, for the rest of the world. Perhaps the most memorable portion of these thirteen verses is the brief segment shown below, in which Isaiah uses a series of animal images—some of them quite familiar—to picture the desolation, devastation, and barrenness of the land, now given over to the wild creatures. The land will lie deserted for generations; even the cities and villages will be inhabited by birds and animals that normally do not live in populated areas.

It shall be a habitation of jackals,
A courtyard for ostriches.
The wild beasts of the desert shall also meet with the
    jackals,
And the wild goat shall bleat to its companion;
Also the night creature shall rest there,

And find for herself a place of rest.
There the arrow snake shall make her nest and lay eggs
And hatch, and gather them under her shadow;
There also shall the hawks be gathered,
Every one with her mate.
(Isa. 34:13–15 NKJV)

esu WHAT IS THE "NIGHT CREATURE"?

Isaiah 34:14 reads:

The wild beasts of the desert shall also meet with the jackals,
And the wild goat shall bleat to its companion;
*Also the **night creature** shall rest there,*
And find for herself a place of rest. (emphasis added)

The word translated "night creature" actually refers to a Mesopotamian demon called Lilith, believed to attack both babies and mothers in childbirth, eating their flesh and sucking their blood. In other words, this passage is saying that God would bring such total destruction to the land of the Edomites, for their hostility to Him, that the most dreaded demon of that era would be perfectly at home in the desolation God would bring about.

THE FUTURE GLORY OF ZION (CHAPTER 35)

Many commentators consider this chapter one of the highlights of the first half of the book of Isaiah. Certainly it is one of the most uplifting, full of memorable lines that—like so many others from Isaiah's pen—found their way into classical pieces, such as the text of Handel's *Messiah*, and even the ordinary speech of people in the streets.

These are some of the promises God makes to His people, to be fulfilled during the millennial kingdom. There is no more fitting tribute to the glory of God, as revealed through His faithful servant Isaiah, than simply to read these moving words, unhampered by blank lines and unencumbered by commentary:

> Then the eyes of the blind shall be opened,
> And the ears of the deaf shall be unstopped.
> Then the lame shall leap like a deer,
> And the tongue of the dumb sing.
> For waters shall burst forth in the wilderness,
> And streams in the desert.
> The parched ground shall become a pool,
> And the thirsty land springs of water;
> In the habitation of jackals, where each lay,
> There shall be grass with reeds and rushes.
>
> A highway shall be there, and a road,
> And it shall be called the Highway of Holiness.
> The unclean shall not pass over it,
> But it shall be for others.
> Whoever walks the road, although a fool,
> Shall not go astray.
> No lion shall be there,
> Nor shall any ravenous beast go up on it;
> It shall not be found there.
> But the redeemed shall walk there,
> And the ransomed of the LORD shall return,
> And come to Zion with singing,
> With everlasting joy on their heads.
> They shall obtain joy and gladness,
> And sorrow and sighing shall flee away.
> (Isa. 35:5–10 NKJV)

OF BIBLICAL "DAYS OF RECKONING"

We sometimes tend to think of the ancient prophets as purveyors of doom and gloom, who spoke incessantly of judgment and condemnation. In doing so, we forget that the rest of the Old Testament is filled with stories of "days of reckoning" for various people. Think of the proud pharaoh of Moses' time, whose army drowned in the Red Sea; of King Saul, who let jealousy of David consume his kingship; of Jezebel, whose contempt for God eventually got her thrown out a window to be eaten by dogs. Or think of the ungrateful rich man, Nabal, who refused to help David and his soldiers even on a feast day; and of so many others who enjoyed huge blessings for a time, only to lose them all in the end.

Another clear example of a "day of reckoning," centering around unwillingness to forgive, occurs in the parable told by Jesus in Matthew 24. This story concerned the man who owed his king ten thousand talents—far more than he could ever pay. So the king, "moved with compassion," forgave the debt and released the debtor. Later that same day the ungrateful man threw a fellow servant into prison for a much smaller debt, at which point the king called him back, reinstated his former debt, and threw him into prison himself.

Perhaps all too often, both history and the prophets simply remind us of realities we'd rather not remember—that sometimes we get what we deserve right here in this lifetime!

PULLING IT ALL TOGETHER . . .

- These two chapters are the first of a half-dozen transitional chapters that separate the two main halves of the book of Isaiah.

- The first is what, by now, seems like a "traditional" judgment; the second is far more hopeful and filled with unforgettable language.

7   INTERMISSION

ISAIAH 36:1–39:8

Before We Begin . . .

What does the concept of an "intermission" mean to you? In what context do we commonly use this word today? What is an intermission's purpose?

If you were Isaiah, would you feel any personal need, or desire, to prove the accuracy of anything you'd already written? If so, how would you propose to do that?

When many students of the Bible encounter chapters 36–39 of Isaiah for the first time, they sometimes wonder what those chapters are doing there. Suddenly, all the judgments and woes against the enemies of God's people, and all the prophecies about eventual blessings on those who remain true to Him, give way to something else entirely.

These four chapters are almost 100 percent historical. In fact, they read a lot like 2 Kings 18–19 and 2 Chronicles 32:1–23, which tell the same stories but were probably written after Isaiah wrote his account. What's going on? Why did Isaiah include two chapters of "pure history" right in the middle of a prophetic book?

Perhaps the best way to understand these chapters is to think of them as a transitional insert between the two main halves of the book of Isaiah. Most scholars believe that Isaiah included chapters 36–37 to "put a cap" on what he'd already written—not so much to prove his own reliability, with respect to the history versus prophecies of his own era, but to prove how trustworthy the Word of God is. Isaiah then included chapters 38–39 to "point forward" to what God had given him to write next.

This assumes, of course, that Isaiah wrote each chapter in sequence, from 1 through 66—which isn't necessarily true! However, the order in which they are arranged makes a great deal of sense. Indeed, to many scholars the logic of putting them exactly where they are is absolute.

Basically, these four chapters give us the main details of two major historical events of Isaiah's time:

The first event, covered in chapters 36–37, involves everything that happened when King Sennacherib of Assyria, whom we have encountered several times already in this study guide, approached Jerusalem with a huge army in 701 BC. He intended to conquer Judah's (and, indeed, all of Israel's) capital city, and then the entire Southern Kingdom as well, exactly as his father, Sargon, had done to the Northern Kingdom a little more than twenty years before.

The second event, covered in chapters 38–39, involves everything that happened when King Hezekiah became ill and found himself facing his own mortality. God literally spared him from death and gave him fifteen additional years of life. However, rather than humbling himself before God throughout his remaining years, King Hezekiah allowed pride and arrogance to enter his life. In so doing, he helped set the stage for the cataclysmic events that would eventually follow.

Now, when you put these two events in perspective (which is a lot easier, of course, if you also know something about what's coming next), you realize that the first event validates everything that Isaiah wrote in the previous thirty-five chapters. And, the second event lays down a foundation for everything coming up in chapters 40–66.

SENNACHERIB INVADES JUDAH (CHAPTER 36)

Chapter 36 begins with the two verses below. Fill in the blanks to see how all this started:

> *Now it came to pass in the fourteenth year of King Hezekiah that Sennacherib king of Assyria came up against all the _____ cities of Judah and took them. Then the king of Assyria sent the Rabshakeh with a great army from Lachish to King Hezekiah at Jerusalem. And he stood by the _____ from the upper pool, on the highway to the Fuller's Field. (Isa. 36:1–2 NKJV)*

In other words, although the Bible does not mention what route Sennacherib took, other sources tell us that he came from the north, along the western edge of the Mediterranean Sea, conquering all the small towns and villages along the way. He then sent his field commander (Rabshakeh) to Jerusalem, along with a "great army," all of whom then stopped just outside the city. By what many scholars do not believe to be coincidence, the Assyrian troops stopped at the same aqueduct where Isaiah had been sent to counsel King Ahaz, the former king of Judah, when Ahaz was facing a similar challenge in chapter 7 of Isaiah.

WAS IT A MAN OR A TITLE?

At least one translation of the Bible renders the word *Rabshakeh,* wherever it appears in both Isaiah and 2 Kings, as "field commander." Others, such as the NKJV, treat it as a proper name preceded by "the." The comparable English construction would be "the Edward" or "the Charles." Still other translations render it as "cupbearer," "field marshall," or "chief of staff." Obviously, the correct translation for this obscure word is still in dispute.

Read the remainder of chapter 36 and answer the following questions:

What was the Rabshakeh's basic message to the envoys King Hezekiah sent to negotiate with him?

What was the overall tone of that message?

What did the Rabshakeh mean, specifically, when he referred to "this broken reed, Egypt" (v. 6)? What did Egypt have to do with any of this?

In verse 8, what was the further insult he offered to the soldiers of Hezekiah's army, charged with defending their city?

How would you feel if you were a soldier, hearing this particular mockery?

How did King Hezekiah's soldiers respond?

What did the Rabshakeh imply, in verse 12, that the men on the wall would eventually have to do if King Hezekiah refused to concede?

GOD RESCUES JUDAH (CHAPTER 37)

Everything that happened in chapter 36 might be considered the opening act of a six-part drama. Parts two through six then occurs in chapter 37, as follows:

In part two, when Hezekiah learned what Sennacherib's field commander had said, he tore his clothes (see "Why Did They Wreck Their Clothes?" on page 72) and sent envoys to Isaiah, asking Isaiah to pray for Jerusalem's deliverance. Fill in the blanks in the passage below to see how Isaiah responded:

Thus you shall say to your _____, "Thus says the
LORD: 'Do not be afraid of the _____ which you
have heard, with which the _____ of the king of
_____ have _____ Me. Surely I will send
a spirit upon him, and he shall hear a _____ and
return to his own land; and I will cause him to fall by
the _____ in his own land.' " (Isa. 37:6–7 NKJV)

WHY DID THEY WRECK THEIR CLOTHES?

The Bible contains many references to the practice of tearing one's clothes. This was a traditional sign of mourning, undertaken at the death of someone beloved, but in this case it was undertaken by Hezekiah at the news of the Assyrian's army's arrival—which might be taken as a sign of impending death. Examples of other biblical characters who tore their clothes in grief include Jacob at the presumed death of Joseph, King David and all the men with him at the deaths of Saul and Jonathan, and Job at the deaths of his children.

The Jewish term *kriah* now covers this ancient practice, still honored in modern times. However, some modern funeral homes, at Jewish funerals, supply black ribbons to be affixed to the clothes and then torn symbolically. Given the price of a modern suit—and the difficulty of getting one fixed and like new again—this certainly makes sense.

In part three, Sennacherib's field commander returned to where Sennacherib was still fighting, at Libnah. Then came to him a rumor that the king of Ethiopia was making war against him and needed to be dealt with—exactly as God had promised. At that point Sennacherib sent a final delegation of messengers to Hezekiah, bearing a letter that Sennacherib probably thought of as his final ultimatum, which also repeated the insults against Israel's God that his field commander had already made. And, of course, it strongly suggested that Hezekiah's God could not possibly defend him any more than the numerous lowercase gods of the people Sennacherib had already conquered could defend them.

In part four, Hezekiah went to the temple, spread Sennacherib's letter out before God, and prayed for salvation for himself, the city, and the people.

God's response in part five, spoken by Isaiah, is a long, mocking judgment against Sennacherib that ends with these words:

> *Because your rage against Me and your _____*
> *Have come up to My ears,*
> *Therefore I will put My _____ in your _____*
> *And My bridle in your _____,*
> *And I will turn you back*
> *By the way which you came.*
> *(Isa. 37:29 NKJV)*

In part six, as mentioned earlier in this study guide, God sent an angel of death to kill 185,000 of Sennacherib's soldiers during the night. Sennacherib then went home, exactly as God had promised he would. Not long after that he was killed by two of his own sons, in the very act of worshiping a false god called Nisroch. Here is Isaiah's account of how Sennacherib's life ended:

> *Now it came to pass, as he [Sennacherib] was worshiping in the house of Nisroch his god, that his sons Adrammelech and Sharezer struck him down with the sword; and they escaped into the land of Ararat. Then Esarhaddon his son reigned in his place. (Isa. 37:38 NKJV)*

HEZEKIAH'S BIG MISTAKE (CHAPTERS 38–39)

Chapters 38–39 represent another of those instances we have mentioned before, in which the Hebrew writers of Scripture did not always record events in chronological order. From the story itself—and from the mention of Merodach-Baladan (39:1), who ruled before Sennacharib invaded Judah in 701 BC—we know that these events also must have occurred prior to 701 BC.

The story itself is actually quite simple. Read chapter 38, and answer the questions below; then we will conclude with the events of chapter 39.

What is the well-known quote from Isaiah, found in Isaiah 38:1?

What emotion does Hezekiah express (vv. 2–3) when he "turned his face to the wall"?

How many years does the Lord promise to "add to Hezekiah's days" in verse 5?

What else does God promise in verse 6?

What extraordinary sign does God give Hezekiah, in verse 8, to prove that He means what He said?

Verses 9–20 then include a song of gratitude and praise, written by Hezekiah, followed by these words of Isaiah, detailing the medical procedures the king's doctors should follow to bring about Hezekiah's healing:

> *Now Isaiah had said, "Let them take a lump of figs, and apply it as a poultice on the boil, and he shall recover." (Isa. 38:21 NKJV)*

The only problem, which no one but God could have foreseen, was that Hezekiah almost immediately felt a rush of pride, apparently in both himself and what he felt were "his" possessions. Not long after he recovered, in chapter 39, he received a delegation of visitors from Babylon, headed by Merodach-Baladan, the son of the then-current king of Babylonia. Because Hezekiah was "pleased with them" (39:2 NKJV), he very unwisely showed them everything of value that they were willing to see, most likely acting as though he owned it all himself even though the temple artifacts, the temple treasury, and other items belonged only to God Himself.

When Isaiah found out what Hezekiah had done, he immediately prophesied two things: first, that what Hezekiah had apparently pretended was his own wealth would all be carried off to Babylon, and second, that some of the king's descendants would wind up serving the king of Babylon. Given that the main threat to Judah at that time seemed to be the Assyrians, both of these prophecies would have been both amazing and upsetting to anyone who heard them, although Hezekiah seemed to take them both in stride.

The chapter ends with the following words:

> *So Hezekiah said to Isaiah, "The word of the LORD which you have spoken is good!" For he said, "At least there will be peace and truth in my days." (Isa. 39:8 NKJV)*

In other words, "Everything is fine as long as disaster waits until I'm gone!"

PULLING IT ALL TOGETHER . . .

- In these chapters, Isaiah takes something of a "time-out" and recaps the history that developed after he'd already written many of the previous chapters.

- In a sense, Isaiah proves his own accuracy—that is, that he not only is a true prophet but can be relied on to reproduce God's instructions faithfully.

- More important, however, Isaiah uses these "in-between" chapters to demonstrate that the words God has given him to put down are 100 percent truthful.

COMFORT AND DELIVERANCE

ISAIAH 40:1–48:22

Before We Begin ...

If you were a citizen of Jerusalem in Isaiah's time and had read what he wrote so far, how do you think you would feel about your own future? About that of your children?

Why do you believe Isaiah (or God) put the chapters focusing on comfort and deliverance toward the end of his book rather than closer to its beginning?

After he finished his four transitional chapters, Isaiah built his remaining twenty-seven chapters around three major, interrelated themes: comfort, deliverance, and restoration. However, that doesn't mean that Isaiah never returned to some of his earlier messages, especially his judgments and woes. Even in this very section of eight chapters, he came back more than once to his condemnation of Babylon. And as before, he often used the classic compare/contrast method to put the blessings and mercies of God in stark relief against the far darker nature of humanity in general.

Even so, the shift in emphasis and tone is clear and distinct, beginning with the very first words of chapter 40: "Comfort, yes, comfort My people!" Let us consider each chapter in order.

COMFORT FOR GOD'S PEOPLE (CHAPTER 40)

Please read the entire text of chapter 40, then answer the following questions:

What does the Lord say has ended? What has been pardoned?

For whom has this been done? That is, who does "Jerusalem" represent?

What New Testament person do you think became "the voice of one crying in the wilderness"?

To whom do the words "all flesh," in verses 5 and 6, refer?

Where are God's people told to "get up into"?

In verse 10, how is the expression "His arm" used? Have you encountered it anywhere else in the Bible?

Where has God "measured the waters"?

Verses 12–14 ask a series of questions. Who is the object of comparison in those questions? And for extra credit, where else in the Bible are these kinds of questions asked and similar comparisons made?

What do you believe is the main message of verses 28–31? That God does what?

A True Treasure Trove . . .

Surely it's impossible, for anyone who has ever heard Handel's *Messiah* more than once (and as we also mentioned in the introduction to this study guide), to fail to notice how many of the words come from the book of Isaiah. Chapter 40 is especially rich—of its first eleven verses, eight are quoted, in whole or in part, in *Messiah* (which, incidentally, does not have a "the" in its title). Here are the verses Handel and his librettist, Charles Jennens, selected from this chapter alone, taken here from the familiar King James Version of the Bible.

Comfort Ye (Isa. 40:1–3)
Comfort ye, comfort ye my people, saith your God. Speak ye comfortably to Jerusalem, and cry unto her, that her warfare is accomplished, that her iniquity is pardoned: for she hath received of the LORD's hand double for all her sins. The voice of him that crieth in the wilderness, Prepare ye the way of the LORD, make straight in the desert a highway for our God.

Every Valley Shall Be Exalted (Isa. 40:4)
Every valley shall be exalted, and every mountain and hill shall be made low: and the crooked shall be made straight, and the rough places plain.

And the Glory of the LORD (Isa. 40:5)
And the glory of the LORD shall be revealed, and all flesh shall see it together: for the mouth of the LORD hath spoken it.

O Thou That Tellest Good Tidings to Zion (Isa. 40:9)
O Zion, that bringest good tidings, get thee up into the high mountain; O Jerusalem, that bringest good tidings, lift up thy voice with strength; lift it up, be not afraid; say unto the cities of Judah, Behold your God!

He Shall Feed His Flock Like a Shepherd (Isa. 40:11)
He shall feed his flock like a shepherd: he shall gather the lambs with his arm, and carry them in his bosom, and shall gently lead those that are with young.

ISRAEL ASSURED OF GOD'S HELP (CHAPTER 41)

Chapter 41 begins with a challenge from God to the people of all nations to come before Him and make their best case for themselves. He then describes his calling of Cyrus, king of Persia, to act as His own instrument in what was still the distant future for the people of Israel when Isaiah wrote these words. Cyrus was the Persian king who conquered Babylon in 538 BC, nearly fifty years into the Israelites' seventy-year Babylonian captivity. He was also the one who gave them their eventual freedom. Note the bold words in the verses below to see how Isaiah described him:

> Who raised up **one from the east**?
> Who in righteousness called him to His feet?
> Who gave the nations before him,
> And made him rule over kings?
> Who gave them as the dust to his sword,
> As driven stubble to his bow?
> Who pursued them, and passed safely
> By the way that **he had not gone with his feet**?
> (Isa. 41:2–3 NKJV, emphasis added)

Who takes rightful credit, in verse 4 of this chapter, for all of the above?

Verses 8–10 are often cited to show how "personal" God is toward His people and how He loves them and desires to care for them. Fill in the blanks in the following verses to see how vividly He expresses His feelings:

But you, Israel, are My _____,
Jacob whom I have chosen,
The descendants of _____ My friend.
You whom I have taken from the ends of the earth,
And called from its farthest regions,
And said to you, "You are My _____,
I have chosen you and have not cast you away:
Fear not, for I am with you;
Be not _____, for I am your God.
I will strengthen you,
Yes, I will help you,
I will uphold you with My _____ right hand."
(Isa. 41:8–10 NKJV)

esu A SERVANT OR A FRIEND?

How would you feel about being called a servant of God, as in Isaiah 41:8? Is this a compliment or an affront? Would this tend to build up or deplete your personal confidence? Your sense of value?

Many people feel that being called a "servant of God" is the highest compliment and the greatest calling of all. And surely it is, for this is how Moses and several other biblical role models were known. Indeed, the only person who is specifically called a "friend of God" in the Bible (imagine being God's personal friend!), according to several translations, is Abraham as recorded in James 2:23. He was also known as "Abraham, My friend" as shown in Isaiah 41:8, and in 2 Chronicles 20:7 as "Abraham Your friend" when the writer addressed his words directly to God.

Chapter 41 follows the above verses by showing how God is the Israelites' helper and redeemer and how He will care for the poor and needy (vv. 17–20). He then refers to Cyrus once again, this time calling him "one from the north" as shown in the following:

I have raised up one from the north,
And he shall come;
From the _____ of the sun he shall call on My
*   name;*
And he shall come against princes as though _____,
As the potter treads clay.
(Isa. 41:25 NKJV)

This might seem confusing, since he was called "from the east" in verse 2, but Cyrus was born in the east (Persia) yet approached Babylon from the north by conquering Media first.

THE SERVANT OF THE LORD (CHAPTER 42)

Isaiah uses the word *servant* to refer to three different entities within these nine chapters—Cyrus, the nation of Israel, and Christ the Messiah. In this chapter he uses it in the first verse to reference Christ, as follows:

Behold! My Servant whom I uphold,
My Elect One in whom My soul delights!
I have put My Spirit upon Him;
He will bring forth justice to the Gentiles.
(Isa. 42:1 NKJV)

In the next three verses (2–4) alone, in how many different ways does Isaiah tell us that Christ, the Son, will be a servant to the Father? List them in the space below.

In the next five verses (5–9) alone, in how many different ways does God demonstrate His power? How many things does He promise to do for His people? List all the "ways" and "things" you can find in the space below.

Who do you believe is the "servant" mentioned in verse 19— Christ or the nation of Israel? Why?

Verse 24 again refers to Israel, recounting one more time a few of their sins. Fill in the blanks below:

> *Who gave Jacob for _____, and Israel to the robbers?*
> *Was it not the LORD,*
> *He against whom we have sinned?*
> *For they would not _____ in His _____,*
> *Nor were they _____ to His law.*
> *(Isa. 42:24 NKJV)*

THE REDEEMER OF ISRAEL (CHAPTER 43)

Chapter 43 can be broken down into at least four sections, as follows:

SECTION 1 (vv. 1–7)

In this section God brings tender assurance to His people. Please read it and in the space provided list as many of the things He either has done or will do for them.

SECTION 2 (vv. 8–13)

In this section God summons Israel and "all the nations" (v. 9) to a test of His omnipotence. Of particular significance is this verse, below:

> *Indeed before the day was, I am He;*
> *And there is no one who can deliver out of My hand;*
> *I work, and who will reverse it?*
> *(Isa. 43:13 NKJV)*

According to this verse, which came first—the "day" or the Lord? Does this line up with what we are told in Genesis?

SECTION 3 (vv. 14–21)

In this section the Lord again speaks of what He will do one day to Babylon. He then concludes with these words; please fill in the blanks to see what they are.

> *I will even make a _____ in the wilderness*
> *And _____ in the desert.*
> *The _____ of the field will honor Me,*
> *The jackals and the _____,*
> *Because I give waters in the wilderness*
> *And rivers in the desert,*
> *To give drink to My people, My chosen.*
> *This people I have formed for Myself;*
> *They shall _____ My praise.*
> *(Isa. 43:19–21 NKJV)*

SECTION 4 (VV. 22–28)

The last section of this chapter begins with a brief reference to Israel as she was in the days before her captivity. It then ends with another promise to deliver the people in spite of their sin, which began with Adam ("your first father") and continued even to that moment.

GOD'S BLESSING ON ISRAEL (CHAPTER 44)

Chapter 44 continues with the Lord's list of blessings that He will pour out on His people. Especially touching is the series of names He uses for His people—"Jacob My servant" (there's that word again!), Israel, and Jeshurun, the last two of which mean "prince of God" and "upright." Read through this chapter, then answer the following questions, for each of which the verse notation is included.

On whom will God pour out water (v. 3)?

Who will spring up like willows by the watercourses (vv. 3–4)?

Who is the First and the Last (v. 6)?

In verse 11, who are called "mere men"? What are they doing? For whom?

Who works with tongs and hammers (v. 12)?

Read Isaiah 44:9–20. This is one of the most memorable parts of this chapter—perhaps even somewhat funny; surely it details the kind of thing the Lord must sometimes laugh at! But what does it refer to—what practice of the pagans (and sometimes the Israelites as well) is the Lord mocking in this passage? Does what He says "ring true"? Why do you suppose people are actually willing (and sometimes even eager!) to pursue the folly that God describes in these verses?

Who does God call "My shepherd" who will "perform My pleasure" (v. 28)?

GOD'S MOST UNLIKELY INSTRUMENT (CHAPTER 45)

Chapter 45 demonstrates something that most longer-term believers have found to be true in their own lives, if they've really put their trust in God for any length of time. God can literally use anything and anyone to achieve His ends, no matter who or what they might be. In this case He used Cyrus, a pagan conqueror, first to defeat the Babylonians and then to free God's own people from captivity a few years later.

Why does God call Cyrus "His anointed" in verse 1?

In verse 2, the Lord says He will go before Cyrus and "make the crooked places straight." Who else did He promise to do that for in chapter 40? Why, then, would He do the same thing for Cyrus?

In verse 3, what might the Lord mean when He says He will give Cyrus the "treasures of darkness"?

Verse 7 has been misunderstood more than once! Which do you believe it means—that God Himself creates calamity of His own volition, or that He allows us to do so via our own selfish desires and inclinations?

What does the Lord say in verse 13 that directly and unmistakably "nails it" with respect to His use of Cyrus to achieve His own ends?

In the remainder of chapter 45, verses 14–25, God proclaims that Israel's enemies will one day come to her and bow down, and that He purposely created the world not "in vain" but to be inhabited. He then challenges those who worship idols to prove that their gods can know the future as He does.

Please fill in the blanks in the following passage to see how He ends the chapter:

I have sworn by Myself;
The _____ has gone out of My mouth in
*   righteousness,*
And shall not return,
That to Me every knee shall bow,
Every _____ shall take an oath.
He shall say, "Surely in the LORD I have _____
*   and strength.*
To Him men shall come,
And all shall be _____
Who are _____ against Him.
In the LORD all the descendants of Israel
Shall be justified, and shall glory."
(Isa. 45:23–25 NKJV)

DEAD IDOLS VS. THE LIVING GOD (CHAPTER 46)

Verses 1–2 of this relatively short chapter identify two pagan idols, Bel and Nebo, neither of whom would have the power to prevent themselves from being carried off into captivity in Babylon when the time came. This sets the tone for the rest of the chapter, in which God makes it very clear—as in chapter 44—that it simply is not possible to compare handmade idols with the one true God Himself. How absurd—the very men and women who worship false gods create them first!

Fill in the blanks in the following two-verse passage with which Isaiah ends this chapter.

Listen to Me, you stubborn-hearted,
Who are far from _____:
I bring My _____ near, it shall not be far off;

My salvation shall not linger.
And I will place _____ in Zion,
For Israel My glory.
(Isa. 46:12–13 NKJV)

THE HUMILIATION OF BABYLON (CHAPTER 47)

Chapter 47 concentrates on Babylon, detailing how she too will eventually be brought low. God says that He will do this for four reasons.

First, though God used the Babylonians to punish His own people, He did not sanction their cruelty, especially against the elderly.

Second, from the successes that He allowed, the Babylonians became proud and arrogant, and few things anger God more than false pride.

Third, the Babylonians trusted in every false god they could invent rather than the one true God.

Fourth, the Babylonians moved beyond false pride to blind conceit about their own abilities.

To see how these observations play out, please read the entire chapter and then answer the following questions.

In verse 6, what does God say that the Babylonians "laid very heavily" on the elderly among His people?

What did the Babylonians say about themselves in verse 8?

In verse 9, why does God say that the "loss of children" and "widowhood" would come upon them?

What do the Babylonians say about themselves in verse 10?

Fill in the blanks below in the last verse from this chapter.

> *Thus shall they be to you*
> *With whom you have labored,*
> *Your _____ from your youth;*
> *They shall _____ each one to his quarter.*
> *No one shall _____ you.*
> *(Isa. 47:15 NKJV)*

ISRAEL REFINED FOR GOD'S GLORY (CHAPTER 48)

In chapter 48, God speaks directly to His people once again. As He so often does, He patiently reviews their history with Him, then explains what He intends to do. Here is how this chapter is organized.

First, God addresses His people as though they were already in Babylon. He points out their obvious apostasies—they "make mention of the God of Israel, but not in truth or in right-eousness" (v. 1); they "call themselves after the holy city [Jerusalem], and lean on the God of Israel" (v. 2), yet they have not been willing to assume the responsibilities of true citizens of God's kingdom—to worship Him as He has so many times directed them.

Second, God makes it clear that He predicted well in advance the events that had then overtaken them. "I have declared the former things from the beginning," He says (v. 3), "lest you should say, 'My idol has done them' " (v. 5). In other words, He repeatedly held them accountable to recognize and acknowledge that He is truly their God. Even so, true to form, they still prefer to credit their idols instead for anything good that happens. But God does not allow them to avoid the truth.

Next, God predicts their eventual return back to Jerusalem, but then explains that He will bring all this about not for their sake but for His own, for "I will not give My glory to another" (v. 11).

Finally, in the closing verses of this chapter, the Lord appeals to His people to "go forth from Babylon" and "say, 'The LORD has redeemed His servant Jacob!' " (v. 20). He ends with this familiar quotation: " 'There is no peace,' says the LORD, 'for the wicked' " (v. 22).

Before we leave this section, please read the verse below and answer the question that follows.

> *Come near to Me, hear this:*
> *I have not spoken in secret from the beginning;*
> *From the time that it was, I was there.*
> *And now the Lord GOD and His Spirit*
> *Have sent Me.*
> *(Isa. 48:16 NKJV)*

Who do you believe the Lord is referring to in the last line when He says "Have sent Me"? (Before you answer, note that He has already identified "the Lord GOD and His Spirit" in the preceding line.)

Finally, please refer to verses 17–22 and answer the following questions.

What are the three ways in which God is referred to in verse 17?

What two things does He do for His people in the same verse?

What does the Lord compare "peace" to in verse 18?

What does He compare righteousness to in the same verse? Also, what is the "sense" of this verse—how should righteousness be "like" what He compares it to?

Finally, what is the proclamation He commands His people to "utter to the end of the earth" in verse 20?

Pulling It All Together . . .

- In chapter 40, Isaiah writes powerfully and extensively of comfort for the nation of Israel. In doing so he also refers repeatedly to the coming Messiah.

- In these chapters, through Isaiah God also points out the vast differences between Himself and the false idols that the people of Isaiah's time still continued to worship.

- God further demonstrates how easy it is for Him to use—literally—anyone He wants to use to achieve His divine ends. This even included the pagan Babylonians and their Assyrian conqueror, Cyrus.

- As always, God did what He did to glorify Himself and make it plain, to all the peoples of the earth, that He is who He says He is—and will always remain the same! That is, the eternal, omnipotent, all-knowing, all-seeing, one and only Creator and Sustainer of the universe.

9   THE SUFFERING SERVANT

ISAIAH 49:1–57:21

Before We Begin ...

When you hear the terms "restoration of the Jews" or "return of the remnant," to what historical event (or events) do you think those words refer?

Who was the "Suffering Servant"? Why was He made to suffer? What was the main result of that suffering?

Much of the previous nine-chapter segment of Isaiah dealt with God's plan to use the Assyrian conqueror, Cyrus, to free His people from their Babylonian captivity. This happened in 516 BC, when a remnant came back to Jerusalem under Ezra's leadership, rebuilt the temple, and reestablished God's people as a sovereign nation of Israel once again.

Thus God ended the Jews' punishment for years of apostasy and restored them to their own land. But God never intended that particular "restoration" to be the final one. Always and forever, the Lord has had a far more complete, far more comprehensive restoration in mind—the full and final restoration of His people to Himself.

For this reason He sent His own Son, Jesus Christ, who came as the Suffering Servant of these next nine chapters of the book of Isaiah. Christ could not "suffer," of course, unless He was rejected by His own people and made to pay the ultimate price for the sins of all humanity. Thus many of the prophecies of Isaiah and the plans of the Lord were fulfilled as one, through the birth and death of Christ, hundreds of years after Isaiah wrote of them in his book. Also, more of those same prophecies and plans continue to be fulfilled, even as God "works them out" through current events and those of the future—a future not quite so distant anymore.

These chapters can be grouped into four sections, as the following discussion will make clear.

MESSIAH AS THE LIGHT TO THE GENTILES (CHAPTERS 49–50)

Please read Isaiah 49:1–6 and answer the following questions.

From where does the speaker, in verse 1, say that the LORD has called him?

Have you ever heard of a biblical reference to "words" and "mouth" and "sharp sword" before? If so, to whom did those allusions apply?

In verse 3, to whom do you think the words "My servant, O Israel" actually apply? Is it the nation of Israel, or is it the same person referred to above, in whom God "will be glorified" in verse 3?

Based on what we have learned so far, who do you believe is speaking in these six verses?

The next section of chapter 49 covers some of the details of Christ's life—how He was rejected by His own people in verse 7 and how God raised Him from the dead and assigned Him the task of bringing His people back to the land of Israel in the millennial kingdom (vv. 8–13).

Chapter 49 then concludes with a long series of interchanges between God and His people. Please fill in the blanks in these two verses, with which the chapters ends:

> *But thus says the LORD:*
> *"Even the _____ of the mighty shall be taken*
>   *away,*
> *And the prey of the _____ be delivered;*
> *For I will contend with him who _____ with you,*
> *And I will save your children.*
> *I will feed those who _____ you with their own*
>   *flesh,*
> *And they shall be drunk with their own _____ as*
>   *with sweet wine.*
> *All flesh shall know*
> *That I, the LORD, am your Savior,*
> *And your _____, the Mighty One of Jacob."*
> *(Isa. 49:25–26 NKJV)*

Messiah begins speaking again in chapter 50. Read verses 4–9 and answer the following questions.

What has the Lord God opened (v. 5)?

What does Messiah say He is not (v. 5)?

To whom does Messiah say that He gave His back (v. 6)?

What does Messiah say that those who fear the Lord and obey the voice of His Servant should do (v. 10)?

THE RIGHTEOUS RULER (51:1–52:12)

In these two chapters the Lord begins by reminding His people of their origins—how He took them from the rock from which they were hewn, which undoubtedly refers to the land from which the Lord called Abraham and Sarah. He then speaks again of the millennial kingdom, at which time all the peoples of the world will wait on His justice. Beginning in verse 12, He then speaks another message of comfort to His people, telling them not to fear any "man who will die" (meaning any mortal person).

Please read these chapters and respond to the following questions.

What does He say has "gone forth" (v. 5)?

In what way will the heavens vanish away (v. 6)?

What will eat up men like a garment (v. 8)? What will eat them like wool?

Who "shall return" (v. 11)?

What does the Lord say His people have drunk the dregs of (v. 17)?

Chapter 51 ends with the following verses. Please fill in the blanks.

Thus says your Lord,
The LORD and your God,
Who pleads the cause of His _____:

"See, I have taken out of your _____
The cup of _____,
The dregs of the cup of My fury;
You shall no longer _____ it.
But I will put it into the hand of those who _____
*   you,*
Who have said to you,
'Lie down, that we may _____ over you.'
And you have laid your body like the _____,
And as the _____, for those who walk over."
(Isa. 51:22–23 NKJV)

The first twelve verses of chapter 52 complement the above—they include a call to Zion to awake from its sleep of captivity and put on its "beautiful garments." Most commentators interpret this as a call to return and rebuild Jerusalem and as a guarantee that the "uncircumcised and unclean" will never again invade the Holy City in the millennial kingdom.

The remainder of chapter 51, beginning with verse 13, belongs to the next section of Isaiah.

EXALTATION OF THE SERVANT (52:13–53:12)

This section of Isaiah deals with Christ as the Suffering Servant, the sin-bearing sacrifice who underwent a terrible death to grant humanity forgiveness for sin. Some commentators even note that He endured all five of the different kinds of wounds known to medical science—contusions, lacerations, penetrating wounds, perforating wounds, and incised wounds.

As you read this section, you will come across one of the most familiar passages in all of Isaiah. We have reproduced it below, with fill-in blanks to help you make sure you read it very carefully. But before you copy the right words from your Bible, see how many blanks you can fill in from memory!

He is despised and _____ by men,
A Man of sorrows and _____ with grief.
And we hid, as it were, our faces from Him;
He was _____, and we did not esteem Him.

Surely He has _____ our griefs
And carried our _____;
Yet we esteemed Him stricken,
Smitten by God, and _____.
But He was wounded for our _____,
He was _____ for our iniquities;
The _____ for our peace was upon Him,
And by His stripes we are _____.
All we like _____ have gone astray;
We have turned, every one, to his own _____;
And the LORD has laid on Him the _____ of
    us all.

He was oppressed and He was afflicted,
Yet He opened not His mouth;
He was led as a _____ to the slaughter,
And as a sheep before its shearers is silent,
So He opened not His mouth.
He was taken from prison and from _____,
And who will declare His generation?
For He was cut off from the land of the _____;
For the _____ of My people He was stricken.
(Isa. 53:3–8 NKJV)

UNDER THE RADAR

When some modern believers in the deity of Christ read the book of Isaiah and compare Isaiah's prophesies with the reality of Christ's life on earth, they find it hard to understand why so many people of Jesus' own time were unable to accept Him as their promised Messiah. One thing that might have made their rejection more likely was the existence, in ancient times, of two or three different conceptions of what the coming Messiah would look like. Some expected a conquering hero and glorious king who would come in dazzling splendor mixed with military might, obliterating their enemies, setting up a divine kingdom, and ushering in world peace. They simply were not looking for an anonymous baby, born in a stable, spending His first night in a feeding trough for camels and donkeys.

Others believed in two separate comings—first as a suffering servant, and second as a glorious king. Perhaps inevitably, over time the conquering hero conception took on more and more appeal until the suffering servant prophecies almost disappeared from their collective memory. In addition, the reality that Christ arose anonymously, "from the people," undoubtedly made Him that much harder to identify by the casual observer. Then too, only in retrospect does the nature of His "suffering servant" persona fall into such stark relief. Hindsight is always clearer.

SALVATION IN THE MILLENNIUM (CHAPTERS 54–57)

These four chapters deal with Christ, the Messiah, in three of His roles in the end times—Redeemer/Restorer, Evangelist to the World, and final Judge of the Wicked. Please read this whole section and answer the following questions, keyed to each chapter.

CHAPTER 54

What will the descendants of the nation of Israel inherit (v. 3)?

To whom and what is verse 5 referring when it says "your Maker is your husband"?

To what does God compare His promise not to be angry with His people (v. 9)?

Who "blows the coals in the fire" (v. 16)?

Chapter 55

Who should come to the waters (v. 1)? What is the price of doing so?

What should the "wicked" and the "unrighteous" forsake (v. 7)?

Fill in the blanks for verse 8, another extremely familiar passage:

> "For My _____ are not your thoughts,
> Nor are your ways My _____," says the LORD.
> (Isa. 55:8 NKJV)

CHAPTER 56

Does the "blessed man" of verse 2 do only what is in that verse, or does he also do what is in verse 1?

To whom does God promise to give the blessings of verse 5? Do you believe that the physical condition of these people will be relevant when this promise is fulfilled?

What will God's house be called (v. 7)?

In verses 9–11, what six things does God call those to whom these verses refer (believed by most commentators to be Israel's irresponsible leaders)?

1.

2.

3.

4.

5.

6.

What do these same people promise to bring (and do!) in verse 12?

CHAPTER 57

In verse 6, what practice does pouring a "drink offering" and making a "grain offering" refer to? What people were once instructed to do this? In this reference, does God find comfort in these things? Why or why not?

Throughout the Old Testament (and the New Testament as well), God compares His desired relationship with His people to a marriage. Given that background, what is God saying in verse 8 of this chapter of Isaiah? Also, to extend this forward, what do you believe will be the general nature of the relationship between God and His people throughout eternity?

In verse 21 (another extremely familiar passage), for whom does God say "there is no peace"?

Proof That Isaiah Was Right

The following table lists some of the prophecies of Isaiah, with respect to the Suffering Servant of chapters 52–53, together with their fulfillment as detailed in the New Testament.

Isaiah's Prophecies as Fulfilled in Christ

Prophecy	Fulfillment
He would be widely rejected (Isa. 53:1, 3).	Jesus "came to His own, and His own did not receive Him" (John 1:11). Also consider John 12:37–38.
He would be disfigured by suffering (Isa. 52:14; 53:2).	Pilate had Jesus beaten. Roman soldiers also put a crown of thorns on His head, struck Him on the head with a stick, and spat on Him (Mark 15:15, 17, 19).
He would voluntarily accept the pain, suffering, and death that sinners deserve (Isa. 53:7–8).	As the Good Shepherd, Jesus laid down His life for His sheep (John 10:11). Also consider John 19:30.
He would make atonement for sin through His blood (Isa. 52:15).	Believers are redeemed and saved through the blood of Christ (1 Pet. 1:18–19).
He would take upon Himself the grief of human sin and sorrow (Isa. 53:4–5).	Jesus was "delivered up because of our offenses" (Rom. 4:25). He "bore our sins in His own body on the tree," and by His stripes we were healed (1 Pet. 2:24–25).
He would die on behalf of "the iniquity [sin] of us all" (Isa. 53:6).	God made Jesus "who knew no sin to be sin for us" (2 Cor. 5:21).

PROOF THAT ISAIAH WAS RIGHT (CONT.)

Prophecy	Fulfillment
He would die to make "intercession for the transgressors" (Isa. 53:12).	Jesus was crucified between two robbers (Mark 15:27–28). Also consider Luke 22:37. He is also called the "one Mediator between God and men" (1 Tim. 2:5).
He would be buried in a rich man's tomb (Isa. 53:9).	Joseph of Arimathea placed the body of Jesus in a new tomb intended for his own eventual use (John 19:38–42).
He would be "exalted and extolled and be very high" (Isa. 52:13).	God has "highly exalted Him and given Him the name" of Lord, to whom "every knee should bow" (Phil. 2:9–11).
He would bring salvation to those who believed in Him (Isa. 53:10–11).	Jesus promised that whoever believes in Him would not perish but have everlasting life (John 3:16). Also consider Acts 16:31.

PULLING IT ALL TOGETHER . . .

• This section of the book of Isaiah concentrates on Christ the Messiah, portrayed as the Suffering Servant who would one day give His life for the sins of humanity.

• Some verses refer to the end times, when He will return to rule as the sovereign of all the earth for one thousand years.

• Throughout all the dialogue of these chapters, God repeatedly demonstrates that He desires His people to remain faithful to Him, to be the pure Bride He speaks of so often in this and other books of both the Old and New Testaments.

RESTORATION

Before We Begin . . .

Based on all you have learned about the book of Isaiah to this point, what would you expect the final chapters to focus on? Why?

What is your concept of the phrase "millennial kingdom"?

The last nine chapters of the book of Isaiah make one thing very clear, both for the people of Isaiah's time and for all those who came later: People are not capable of righteousness on their own. If God's people are to be restored to Him, the initiative must come from God; it simply cannot happen any other way.

In truth, this "message" is infused into the very fabric of the Bible, from Genesis to Revelation. This section of Isaiah simply makes that message even clearer and more dramatic and memorable than it might otherwise be.

Again, this section breaks down naturally into four divisions, each of which is dealt with separately in the remainder of this chapter.

THE COMING RESTORATION (CHAPTERS 58–60)

This section is somewhat like an abbreviated "story of redemption," beginning with what pleases God (chapter 58), dealing with how corruption separates us from Him (chapter 59), and moving on to the future glory of Zion (chapter 60). Please read each chapter separately and then answer the questions below.

CHAPTER 58

In verse 2, what does God say that a righteous nation takes delight in doing?

What kind of fast does God describe in verse 5? What is His opinion of it?

What kind of fast does He desire (that is, what are His prescribed purposes for a fast?), as indicated in verse 6? How is this different from the previous version?

What are the two titles God gives to people, in verse 12, who meet His requirements for righteousness?

WHAT DOES GOD EXPECT?

Isaiah 58:7–10 contains a fascinating (and sobering!) insight into what an effective "fast to the Lord" might actually involve. Here is how Isaiah breaks out his list of the things He says God expects of us—and the rewards that He says will follow. Note, however, that the entries in column 2 are not necessarily keyed to those in column 1—only that those in #2 "follow" those in #1, in a collective sense.

Do this . . .	And this will be the result . . .
Share your bread with the hungry (v. 7);	then your light shall break forth like the morning (v. 8).
Bring to your house the poor who are cast out (v. 7);	then your healing shall spring forth speedily (v. 8).
When you see the naked, cover him, and do not hide yourself from your own flesh (v. 7),	and your righteousness shall go before you (v. 8).
If you take away the yoke from your midst (v. 9)	the glory of the LORD shall be your rear guard (v. 8).
If you take away the pointing of the finger, and speaking wickedness (v. 9),	then you shall call, and the LORD will answer; you shall cry, and He will say, "Here I am" (v. 9).
If you extend your soul to the hungry and satisfy the afflicted soul (v. 10),	then your light shall dawn in the darkness, and your darkness shall be as the noonday (v. 10).

CHAPTER 59

What has the tongue muttered in verse 3?

Verse 6 makes an interesting point—what do you believe "their webs will not become garments" means? What webs do become garments?

In verse 8, what kind of paths do "they" make? How does this compare to the opening verses of Isaiah 40?

Where has truth fallen in verse 14?

What does God say of His covenant (v. 21) that He will make with those who "turn from transgression" (v. 20)? How long does He say it will last?

CHAPTER 60

Fill in the blanks in the following passage.

> Arise, shine;
> For your _____ has come!
> And the _____ of the LORD is risen upon you.
> For behold, the _____ shall cover the earth,
> And deep darkness the _____;
> But the LORD will arise over you,
> And His _____ will be seen upon you.
> The Gentiles shall come to your _____,
> And kings to the _____ of your rising.
> (Isa. 60:1–3 NKJV)

To whom do you believe the previous verses apply?

What will God glorify, according to verse 7?

What is the significance of "the sons of foreigners shall build up your walls" in verse 10?

What shall "no longer be heard in your land" (i.e., Israel) in verse 18?

What shall the city of Jerusalem, in verse 18, call its walls? Its gates?

COMING OF THE MESSIAH (61:1–63:6)

This section repeats the good news of salvation, then offers an unmistakable assurance of Jerusalem's eventual deliverance. It opens with these familiar words:

The Spirit of the Lord GOD is upon Me,
Because the LORD has anointed Me
To preach good tidings to the poor;
He has sent Me to heal the brokenhearted,
To proclaim liberty to the captives,
And the opening of the prison to those who are bound.
(Isa. 61:1 NKJV)

Please read the remainder of chapter 61 carefully, then locate
the verses in which the following phrases appear:

"day of vengeance of our God"
    Verse _____

"the oil of joy"
    Verse _____

"raise up the former desolations"
    Verse _____

"eat the riches of the Gentiles"
    Verse _____

"you shall have double honor"
    Verse _____

"robbery for burnt offering"
    Verse _____

"covered me with the robe of righteousness"
    Verse _____

"as a bride adorns herself with her jewels"
    Verse _____

"as the earth brings forth its bud"
    Verse _____

Chapter 62

This chapter begins with another familiar quotation:

> For Zion's sake I will not hold My peace,
> And for Jerusalem's sake I will not rest,
> Until her righteousness goes forth as brightness,
> And her salvation as a lamp that burns.
> (Isa. 62:1 NKJV)

It then proceeds through a series of "you shalls," which create together an uplifting picture of Jerusalem in the final days. Please read through this chapter and fill in each of the "you shalls" as found in the following verses.

Verse 2:

Verse 3:

Verse 4a:

Verse 4b:

Verse 12:

In addition to these, of course, are several "shalls" that are included but are not phrased precisely as those above. For example, how many more things that the Lord says "shall" be true for Jerusalem you can find in the remainder of chapter 62? List them and number them in the margin.

This section ends with the first six verses of chapter 63, which remind us of what the Lord has been (and will be) required-by His love for us to do—to destroy His enemies. These verses detail what He will do as He "comes from Edom" wearing red garments, like one who has trampled his enemies in a winepress. Fill in the blanks in the passage below to see how it ends.

> I looked, but there was no one to help,
> And I wondered
> That there was no one to _____;
> Therefore My own arm brought _____ for Me;
> And My own fury, it sustained Me.
> I have _____ down the peoples in My anger,
> Made them _____ in My fury,
> And brought down their _____ to the earth.
> (Isa. 63:5–6 NKJV)

PRAYER AND RESPONSE (63:7–65:25)

This section of the book of Isaiah begins with a remembrance of God's mercy, followed by a prayer of penitence, which together complete chapter 63. This is followed by chapter 64, a prayer for help, while chapter 65 is essentially a response in which God promises punishment for the guilty, then looks ahead to His new creation. Answer the following questions as you read through these chapters.

CHAPTER 63

In verse 8, what kind of children does the Lord speak of?

What two things did God "in His love and in His pity" do for His people in verse 9? When did He do so?

What did He lead them through in verse 13?

What have God's adversaries done in verse 18?

CHAPTER 64

Fill in the missing words below in one of Isaiah's best-known verses, Isaiah 64:6 (NKJV).

But we are all like an unclean thing,

_____ _____ _____ *righteousnesses*

_____ _____ _____

_____ ;

We   all _____ _____ _____

_____ ,

And _____ _____ , _____

_____ _____ ,

Have taken _____ _____ .

How would you characterize the remaining verses (7–12) of this chapter? Does it sound like God's people deserve His help? Have they been faithful to Him?

CHAPTER 65

This chapter, as indicated above, focuses on God's response to the prayers that have just ended. In the first portion, God promises that He will bring punishment to those "who walk in a way that is not good, according to their own thoughts" (v. 2). But then, beginning with verse 8, God begins to find reasons to save His people, even "as the new wine is found in the cluster, and one says, 'Do not destroy it, for a blessing is in it.'"

What do you think God meant by these words? What might be this "blessing" He found in His own people?

Then, once again, beginning in verse 11, God speaks to "those who forsake" Him. In verse 13, He says, "My servants shall eat, but you shall be hungry." Thus "you shall leave your name as a curse to My chosen; for the Lord GOD will slay you" (v. 15).

Finally, the chapter ends with another extended promise, beginning with one more familiar quotation from Isaiah 65:17: "For behold, I create new heavens and a new earth."

Verses 14–24 contain a succession of glorious promises to God's people and also describe what things will be like in the millennial kingdom.

Write down as many of these promises as you can find, in these verses only, in the space below. Six promises would be a bare minimum, but see if you can list even more than that.

Finally, this chapter comes to a close with the following memorable words:

> *"The wolf and the lamb shall feed together,*
> *The lion shall eat straw like the ox,*
> *And dust shall be the serpent's food.*
> *They shall not hurt nor destroy in all My holy*
> *   mountain,"*
> *Says the LORD.*
> *(Isa. 65:25 NKJV)*

A House Is Still a Home

The next-to-last chapter of Isaiah contains the following verses:
They shall build houses and inhabit them;
They shall plant vineyards and eat their fruit.
They shall not build and another inhabit;
They shall not plant and another eat;
For as the days of a tree, so shall be the days of My people,
And My elect shall long enjoy the work of their hands.
(Isa. 65:21–22 NKJV)

This sounds very much like a promise that in the millennial kingdom, we will be given meaningful, productive work to do, including building and planting. How literally should this prophecy be taken? What do you think?

FULFILLMENT (CHAPTER 66)

There could not be, perhaps, a more fitting climax to the book of Isaiah than chapter 66, which describes the millennial kingdom—the focus of so much Christian thought, energy, and hope down through the centuries. It begins by picturing God, sitting on His throne with earth as His footstool, for whom no one can build a place to dwell. For He is the Creator who creates all things; what He values above all else is for His people to be humble and contrite (v. 2).

Despite the upbeat beginning, Isaiah follows these introductory verses with an almost strange evocation of things as they were, not as God wanted them, for so many years, within the hearts of people.

List three of the four things that those with perverse hearts did, in verse 3, even as they pretended to serve God.

What else did the same people do in verse 4?

In verse 7, God says of Israel (in the time of the Millennium), "Before she was in labor, she gave birth; before her pain came, she delivered a male child." What does He mean by this? Is He speaking of a literal birth? Of a literal male child? What do you think?

What does God say He "knows" in verse 18?

What does He say "the nations" (including Pul, Lud, and Tubal) will declare in verse 19?

For what does He say He will take some of the children of Israel in verse 21?

Finally, the book of Isaiah ends with the following words, certainly a suitable culmination of all that has gone before.

"For as the new heavens and the new earth
Which I will make shall remain before Me," says the
    LORD,
"So shall your descendants and your name remain.
And it shall come to pass
That from one New Moon to another,
And from one Sabbath to another,
All flesh shall come to worship before Me," says the
    LORD.
"And they shall go forth and look
Upon the corpses of the men
Who have transgressed against Me.
For their worm does not die,
And their fire is not quenched.
They shall be an abhorrence to all flesh."
(Isa. 66:22–24 NKJV)

COMING TO A CLOSE

By the time you finish the book of Isaiah, you are probably in awe. Whether this is your first, tenth, or hundredth time to read through Isaiah, there can be no doubt that this is an awesome message from an awesome God.

Why that particular word—*awe?* Well, it could probably be justified any number of ways, but let us consider three elements of the book of Isaiah—awesome prophet, awesome message, and awesome God.

AWESOME PROPHET

Though we know comparatively little about Isaiah the man, we certainly know that he was faithful to the task God put before him. And we know that he was a true prophet as well, according to the definition given to Moses in Deuteronomy 18:21–22:

> And if you say in your heart, "How shall we know the word which the LORD has not spoken?"—when a prophet speaks in the name of the LORD, if the thing does not happen or come to pass, that is the thing which the LORD has not spoken; the prophet has spoken it presumptuously; you shall not be afraid of him.

Imagine, if you can, going to kings such as Hezekiah and telling them they are about to die. Imagine delivering the messages of judgment and condemnation Isaiah delivered to the very people he lived with every day, time and time again. Granted, the messages of redemption and resurrection were awesome too, but given what we know about the history of Isaiah's time, it's clear that most of those prophecies were not acted upon and probably not even "heard in the heart" by those for whom they were intended. So Isaiah got little encouragement and much opposition from those around him. Even so, without question he was unwavering, courageous, and completely committed to serving the God who called him above all else.

AWESOME MESSAGE

Much of the message Isaiah delivered has already proven true. Some of that proof came within a few years after he wrote the words—for example, the fall of the Northern Kingdom to Assyria; followed 138 years later by the fall of the Southern Kingdom to Babylon; followed seventy years later by the liberation and return to Jerusalem of the children of Israel, brought about by Cyrus, the Persian conqueror of Babylon—also foretold in awesome detail by Isaiah long before it happened.

Other proof came much later—Christ was born of a virgin, descended from Jesse and David, was rejected by his own people, and triumphed over death.

And finally, more proof is yet to come—it becomes increasingly clear, to those who study the end times (a branch of theology called eschatology), that the world is a lot closer to those end times—and therefore a lot closer to the fulfillment of many of Isaiah's prophecies—than most people seem to realize. Certainly the return of Israel to her own land, in 1948, fits into its own "milestone" category, yet the additional restoration that is still to come has definitely begun, even as you read these words.

And beyond all that, Isaiah delivered his message in such beautiful, inspired language that millions of people down through the centuries have quoted it over and over with an overwhelming sense of—you guessed it!—awe.

Awesome God

Finally, of course, no eyes could have seen a great light, no ears could have been unstopped, no crooked paths made straight, no valleys exalted, no sins made white as snow, no death swallowed up in victory, and no one could mount up with wings as eagles, except for the awesome power, grace, and love of the God who created all these awesome possibilities. He is the true wonder of the book of Isaiah, for the writer of the message is but a servant to the One from whom the message comes.

This above all is how we should think of Isaiah—as a faithful servant, sent from God, to give us a message we dare not despise, ignore, or forget.

HOW TO BUILD YOUR REFERENCE LIBRARY

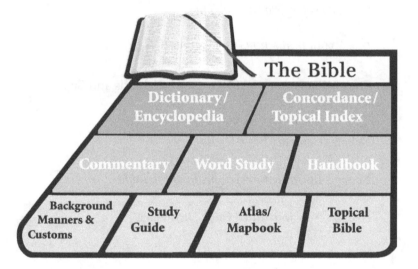

The Bible

Dictionary/ Encyclopedia	Concordance/ Topical Index
Commentary	Word Study	Handbook
Background Manners & Customs	Study Guide	Atlas/ Mapbook	Topical Bible

GREAT RESOURCES FOR BUILDING YOUR REFERENCE LIBRARY

DICTIONARIES AND ENCYCLOPEDIAS

All About the Bible: The Ultimate A-to-Z® Illustrated Guide to the Key People, Places, and Things

Every Man in the Bible by Larry Richards

Every Woman in the Bible by Larry Richards and Sue Richards

Nelson's Compact Bible Dictionary

Nelson's Illustrated Encyclopedia of the Bible

Nelson's New Illustrated Bible Dictionary

Nelson's Student Bible Dictionary

So That's What It Means! The Ultimate A-to-Z Resource by Don Campbell, Wendell Johnston, John Walvoord, and John Witmer

Vine's Complete Expository Dictionary of Old and New Testament Words by W. E. Vine and Merrill F. Unger

CONCORDANCES AND TOPICAL INDEXES

Nelson's Quick Reference Bible Concordance by Ronald F. Youngblood

The New Strong's Exhaustive Concordance of the Bible by James Strong

COMMENTARIES

Believer's Bible Commentary by William MacDonald

Matthew Henry's Concise Commentary on the Whole Bible by Matthew Henry

The MacArthur Bible Commentary by John MacArthur

Nelson's New Illustrated Bible Commentary

Thru the Bible series by J. Vernon McGee

HANDBOOKS

Nelson's Compact Bible Handbook

Nelson's Complete Book of Bible Maps and Charts

Nelson's Illustrated Bible Handbook

Nelson's New Illustrated Bible Manners and Customs by Howard F. Vos

With the Word: The Chapter-by-Chapter Bible Handbook by Warren W. Wiersbe

For more great resources, please visit *www.thomasnelson.com.*

NELSON IMPACT™ STUDY GUIDES

The Finest Study Bible EVER!

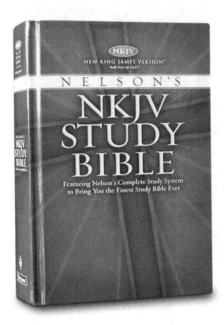

Nelson's NKJV Study Bible helps you understand, apply and grow in a life-long journey through God's Word.

    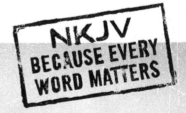

When you want to grow in your faith, Nelson's line of NKJV study tools is all you'll ever need. For more information or to order, contact Thomas Nelson Bibles at 1-800-251-4000 or online at www.nelsonbibles.com

Printed in the USA
CPSIA information can be obtained
at www.ICGtesting.com
LVHW020859210724
785408LV00007B/47